# Forging a West that Works:
## An Invitation to the Radical Center

Essays on Ranching, Conservation, and Science

The Quivira Coalition
April 2003

# Table of Contents

Forging a West that Works:

# Preface

In January of 2003, 20 individuals—ranchers, environmentalists, and scientists—met for 48 hours to figure out a way to reclaim the American West from the decades of divisiveness and acrimony that now truly jeopardize much of what we all love and value. But we also met to take the West forward, to restore ecological, social, and political health to a landscape that so desperately needs it.

We met, in other words, to find a way to make ourselves worthy of the land we all love.

These 20 citizens, drawn from all over the nation, came together in an atmosphere of crisis and hope. All of us believe that the way things are cannot be sustained without the further erosion of life and liberty in the West. And yet all of us believe that positive, regenerative change can, and is, about to happen in what author Wallace Stegner called "the native home of hope."

We set out to write a Declaration and ended up writing an Invitation instead. We wanted to declare an end to the hostilities that have consumed the issue of livestock grazing in the West, hostilities which have failed to protect endangered species and endangered rural communities alike. And we have done that—the call for a cessation to the war between ranchers and environmentalists has been issued.

But after 48 hours of intense but convivial discussions, we also came to the conclusion that peace was not enough. We decided that, to make progress and move forward, we need to mobilize what is being called The Radical Center—a meeting-ground where diverse parties can come to discuss their interests, instead of argue their positions—so as to give purpose, voice, and energy to an effort that has been growing slowly, by fits and starts, over the last decade or so.

In the end, these 20 ranchers, environmentalists, and scientists decided to author and sign an *Invitation to Join the Radical Center,* an invitation that is being widely circulated so that the list of signatories may grow long, varied, and undeniable. Eventually, this Invitation will grow into a campaign, and ultimately, a movement.

This book is a part of that movement.

The essays, written between 1997 and 2002 for The Quivira Coalition—a non-profit organization dedicated to building bridges between ranchers, environmentalists, scientists, state and federal land managers, and concerned members of the public—represent an early effort to construct the Radical

Center. Individually, they focus on practical, innovative, and collaborative solutions to complex natural resource issues in the West. Collectively, they are part of the voice, the ideas, and the sense of hope embodied in the Radical Center.

In these pages, we explore common-sense solutions to the rangeland conflict that should inspire, teach, and provoke others. We do not always agree on the details, nor do any of the authors offer a "silver bullet" to the myriad of challenges confronting this region that we all love, but we all **do** agree to look, learn, listen, and change—where change is necessary—all in the spirit of hope and health for the land and its people.

If you like what you read between these pages, please consider joining us at this meeting ground. Support a watershed group, join a collaborative effort, visit a ranch, buy local food, or read another book. Or sign the Invitation to the Radical Center, included here. (You can sign on at www.quiviracoalition.org.)

The Radical Center is large, diverse, and growing. There is plenty of room for everyone.

Only by linking arms, instead of clenching more fists, will we be able to forge a West that works.

# An Invitation to the Radical Center

For more than 30 years, environmentalists and ranchers have fought over the heart of the American West—the wide open spaces that stretch from our cities to the "purple mountain majesties" we sang of in school.

The combatants have fought long and hard, but as their struggle over the working landscapes of the West pulled in citizens, agency officials, attorneys and judges, one consequence is clear: during the fight, millions of acres of the West's open spaces and biologically rich lands were broken by development.

There have been other unintended consequences. Forest Service and Bureau of Land Management officials who once physically managed our purple mountain majesties now mostly manage mountains of paper. Endangered species hang on by claw or beak despite hundreds of lawsuits. Rural towns simply hang on.

Meanwhile, human communities divide into factions. Most tragically, the stewards of working landscapes are surrendering their lands at unprecedented rates to the pressure which tears the quilt of nature into rags.

Perhaps, the fight had to happen. The West's grasslands and streams and wildlife were in trouble from a century or more of hard use when this fight was joined. The nation had to debate the use of 420,000 square miles of grazed public land across eleven states.

But the fight has gone on far too long. In recent years, the American West has witnessed tremendous positive changes, including the rise of models of sustainable use of public and private lands; the shift of conservation and scientific strategies from "protection" alone to include restoration; and the expanding role of cooperative efforts to move beyond resource conflicts.

As a consequence of these crises and trends we believe it is time to cease hostilities and enter a new era of cooperation.

We believe that how we inhabit and use the West today will determine the West we pass on to our children tomorrow; that preserving the biological diversity of working landscapes requires active stewardship; and that under current conditions the stewards of those lands are compensated for only a fraction of the values their stewardship provides. We know that poor management has damaged land in the past and in some areas continues to do so, but we also believe appropriate ranching practices can restore land to health. We believe that some lands should not be grazed by livestock; but also that much of the West can be grazed in an ecologically sound manner. We know that management practices have changed in recent years, ecological sciences have

generated new and valuable tools for assessing and improving land, and new models of sustainable use of land have proved their worth.

Finally, we believe that the people of the West must halt the further conversion of working landscapes to uses that destroy this wellspring of ecological, aesthetic, and cultural richness which is celebrated around the world.

Time is short. The cost of delay is further irrevocable loss.

We therefore reject the acrimony of past decades that has dominated debate over livestock grazing on public lands, for it has yielded little but hard feelings among people who are united by their common love of land and who should be natural allies.

And we pledge our efforts to form the "Radical Center" where:

•The ranching community accepts and aspires to a progressively higher standard of environmental performance;

•The environmental community resolves to work constructively with the people who occupy and use the lands it would protect;

•The personnel of federal and state land management agencies focus not on the defense of procedure but on the production of tangible results;

•The research community strives to make their work more relevant to broader constituencies;

•The land grant colleges return to their original charters, conducting and disseminating information in ways that benefit local landscapes and the communities that depend on them;

•The consumer buys food that strengthens the bond between their own health and the health of the land;

•The public recognizes and rewards those who maintain and improve the health of all land;

•And that all participants learn better how to share both authority and responsibility.

As the ranks of the Radical Center swell with those who are committed to these goals, the promise increases that "America the Beautiful" may become an image of the future as well as of the past and, with the grace of good fortune, the West may finally create what Wallace Stegner called "a society to match its scenery."

In the expectation that we face a better future for the West we hereby sign our names and invite others to add their own:

**Michael Bean**, conservationist, *Environmental Defense*
**Jim Brown**, ecologist, *University of New Mexico*
**Bob Budd**, *manager of Red Canyon Ranch for The Nature Conservancy*
**Bill deBuys**, author, conservationist, *Director of the Valle Grande Grass Bank*
**Kris Havstad**, *Supervisory Scientist, USDA ARS/Jornada Experimental Range*
**Paul Johnson**, farmer, *former chief, Natural Resources Conservation Service*
**Teresa Jordan**, author
**Daniel Kemmis**, *Center for the Rocky Mountain West*
**Rick Knight**, *professor of wildlife biology, Colorado State University*
**Heather Knight**, *The Nature Conservancy*
**Merle Lefkoff**, mediator
**Bill McDonald**, rancher and *Executive Director, Malpai Borderlands Group*
**Guy McPherson**, ecologist, *University of Arizona*
**Ed Marston**, journalist and *former publisher of High Country News*
**Gary Paul Nabhan**, author and *Director, Center for Sustainable Environments, Northern Arizona University*
**Duke Phillips**, rancher, *Chico Basin Ranch*
**Nathan Sayre**, anthropologist
**Paul Starrs**, *professor of geography, University of Nevada-Reno*
**Bill Weeks**, *The Nature Conservancy*
**Courtney White**, *The Quivira Coalition*

# Introduction:
# Bringing the West Back Home

*by Daniel Kemmis*

The American West has long been viewed, by itself and by others, as standing apart from the rest of the country. Since the early days of the nation's history, the West's distinguishing characteristics and its relationship to the American nation have been subjects of analysis, celebration, misunderstanding, and conflict.

One way of viewing the history of the West is in terms of a very powerful, inspiring, hard, and demanding set of western landscapes creating, over time, a people so fundamentally defined by those places that they must eventually transcend their differences enough to begin exercising a new level of responsibility for their own homeland. I believe that westerners, claimed by and committed to this place, have finally come to the borders of a political maturity that may now enable us to become genuine stewards of the place that made us westerners in the first place.

People who live on a landscape for generations, who have struggled to sustain themselves and their families on its bounty and against its hardships are simply going to have learned lessons about that place that nothing else can teach. But this is seldom how most of the rest of the country sees the West. The roots of those perceptions reach back many decades.

Consider, for example, the way in which Bernard DeVoto's acerbic pen burned into the minds of a small but highly influential segment of America's reading public half a century ago an image of westerners—particularly western ranchers—that still today is a major determinant in public land policy debates. Most non-western environmentalists, for example, remain comfortably convinced that they know everything they need to know about western ranchers—and indeed about westerners in general.

Now, as westerners of many callings—not least among them western ranchers—challenge themselves to find new ways of addressing public land issues, they continue to be haunted by the stinging characterizations of DeVoto and those he influenced. Without denying the considerable extent to which westerners have contributed to that unflattering image, those who genuinely care about the fate of public lands may, for the sake of those lands themselves, need at last to give westerners a chance to prove that they have begun to outgrow their lesser selves. There is now a danger—a very real danger—that the image DeVoto created of the West and of westerners has itself become a western myth, and that it is now keeping both the West and the rest of the country from doing well by western landscapes, communities and ecosystems.

But to be prepared to assume such a role, the West and the nation at large would need to free themselves from old, narrowing and blinding ideologies and myths. In particular, the region needs to be developing modes of thinking radically different from its now often antiquated ways of viewing itself and the rest of the world.

In fact, the West is beginning to understand itself in a new way, as a region with its own cultural identity, an identity strongly shaped by the landforms that define the territory and give shape to its communities. On the ground in dozens of communities, watersheds, and ecosystems throughout the West, something has indeed begun to change. As the region has steadily built a stronger sense of its own identity it has also, at last, begun to outgrow its political infancy by developing a genuinely western way of dealing with western issues.

There is a story almost totally unknown outside the West, but urgently discussed every day now in the western press: the story of a steadily growing number of local agreements among western environmentalists, ranchers, loggers, miners and recreationists about how the public land or natural resources should be managed in their particular river drainage or their ecosystem. The emergence of this indigenous form of western problem-solving is almost precisely what Wallace Stegner had predicted and urged when he spoke of the West "outliving its origins" by learning lessons of cooperation. The collaborative movement, then, is one

crucial dimension of the maturing of the West, but the real historical promise of this movement will only become apparent as the experience of collaborative problem-solving is "brought to scale" by becoming both regional in scope and effectively political in operation.

It is in these terms that I see the "Invitation to Join the Radical Center" as a major step in the maturing of the West. Part of that maturing takes the form of recognizing that many of the battles over western landscapes were very nearly inevitable. In the words of the Invitation, "Perhaps, the fight had to happen. . . .The nation had to debate the use of 420,000 square miles of grazed public land across eleven states. . . .But the fight has gone on far too long."

The language is appropriately reminiscent of that employed by Thomas Paine a few months before the Declaration of Independence when, reviewing the outmoded system of colonial government, he declared, "There was a time when it was proper, and there is a proper time for it to cease." By declaring an end to the old western range wars, those who have signed this invitation have, in effect, declared the beginning of a promising new chapter in the history of the West.

*Daniel Kemmis is the director of the Center for the Rocky Mountain West and the author of* This Sovereign Land, *from which parts of this were drawn.*

# Ranching
# in the Radical Center

*The Malpai Borderlands Group*

# Building the Radical Center

*by William McDonald*

**B**ill McDonald is a rancher in southeastern Arizona and the executive director of the non-profit Malpai Borderlands Group, a ground-breaking collaboration between ranchers, environmentalists, and state and federal land managers with the goal of protecting 800,000 acres of land as a "working wilderness." He is also a recipient of a MacArthur Foundation "genius" Fellowship—the first given to an agriculturalist.

The controversy which has arisen over livestock grazing in the West has been characterized by extreme rhetoric and extreme actions. With government agencies nearly gridlocked and decisive legislation not forthcoming, activists increasingly turn to litigation and sometimes "monkey wrenching" or other forms of intimidation in attempts to force their will upon a process that is often so mired in procedure that even the simplest management actions require reams of supporting paperwork.

Traditionally, the antagonists have been identified as "ranchers vs. environmentalists" or "extractionists vs. conservationists." Not liking the sound of those labels, some prefer "wise-use vs. preservation." Those who graze livestock and their supporters have been expected to line up on one side of the issue, while the environmental community and their supporters line up on the other. Stories in the news media, together with the current spate of litigation over land use, have further solidified the grazing issue in the West as one which is black and white, us against them.

## Consequences for the Land

What is being lost in the rhetoric is the only thing that matters—the eventual consequences for the land. I have purposely avoided the term "public land." In most of the West, the character of the public land depends in a large part on what is taking place on the surrounding and intermingled private lands. Even in areas where the public acreage dwarfs the private, often the private land (the homesteaded land) may contain the only reliable water and/or the easiest ground (open meadow,

---

etc.) for miles. It may be the piece that makes the area work ecologically for the wildlife inhabitants.

If the fate of the public lands depends to some extent on what happens to adjoining private land, it is even surer that the fate of much of the private land depends on the ability of the ranchers who own it to

## Malpai Borderlands Vicinity

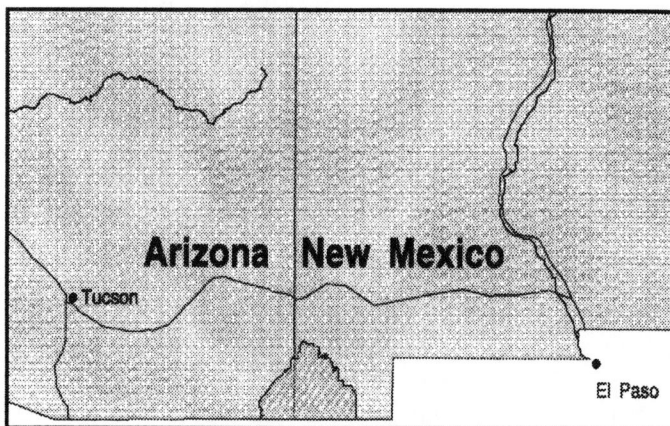

Figure 1. The geographical location of the 782,000-acre planning area of the Malpai Borderlands Group. (Figures 1-4 courtesy of the MBG. All rights reserved.)

graze their cattle on adjoining public land. Denied that ability, many would no longer be able to maintain viable grazing livelihoods. The alternative source of livelihood, in many cases, has been to sell the land to developers.

It was with these concerns in mind that, in 1991, a small group of ranchers in southeastern Arizona and southwestern New Mexico, along the Mexican border, sat down with some folks from the environmental community to break from the traditional stereotypical positions and to try to find common ground, to begin to build, if you will, the "radical center."

At stake was nearly 800,000

acres of unfragmented landscape, the northern tip of the Madrean Archipelago, where Arizona and New Mexico join the Mexican states of Sonora and Chihuahua (Figure 1). As happened in many places in the West, the area had seen a major influx of people and livestock around the turn of the century. The numbers proved to be unsustainable. Fire suppression, overgrazing, and other activities associated with nearly unrestricted settlement exaggerated the effects on the landscape of a climatic regime that is characterized by extremes. Harsh economic reality followed the ecological abuse, causing most to leave in search of other opportunities.

### Two Concerns

Today, about 30 families live on ranches within the huge area, possibly the fewest number of human residents in centuries. The concerns of those who gathered together in 1991 focused on two things.

One was the continuing loss of grasslands to woody species, believed to be partially caused by century-long fire suppression. The other was the anticipated threat of fragmentation of the area from a renewed influx of people. On three sides of the area, subdivision was accelerating. In looking for allies to address these concerns, the ranchers found them in, of all places, the environmental community.

Calling themselves the Malpai Group, the ranchers and their

new-found allies met for discussions in ranch houses over a two-year period. This discussion period had the 320,000-acre Gray Ranch in 1990. They then confounded nearly everyone by selling the property to a

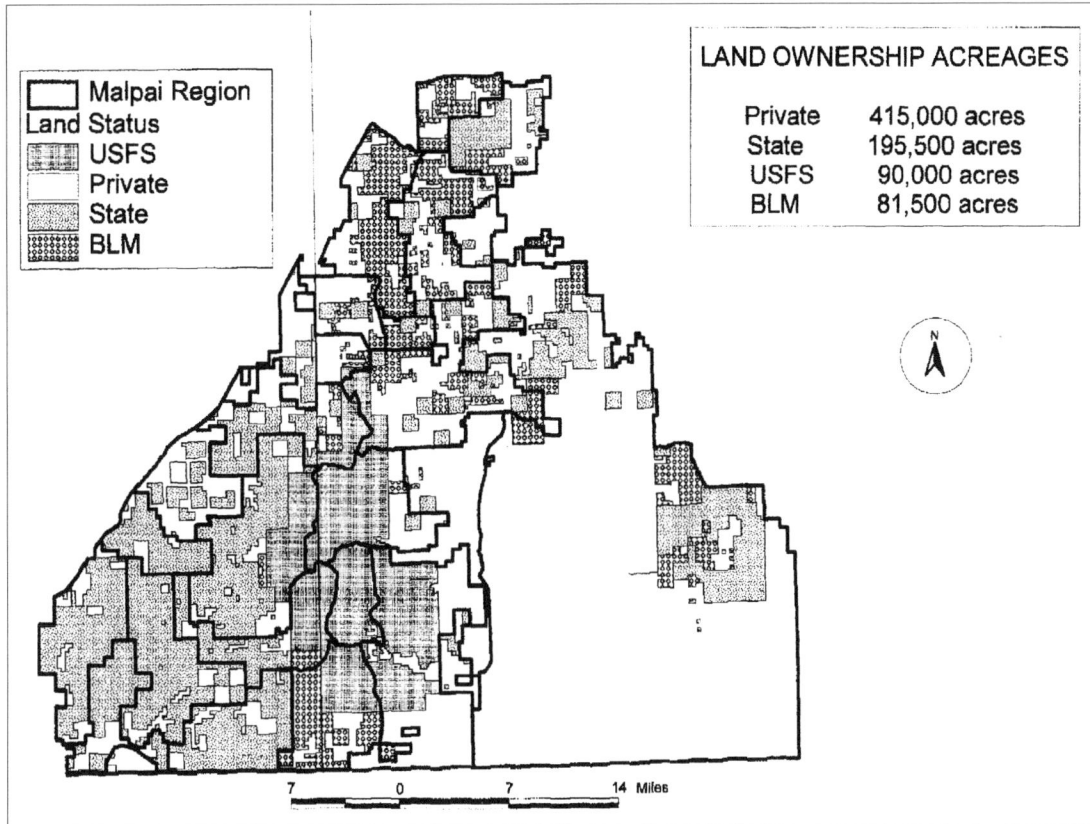

LAND OWNERSHIP ACREAGES

| | |
|---|---|
| Private | 415,000 acres |
| State | 195,500 acres |
| USFS | 90,000 acres |
| BLM | 81,500 acres |

Figure 2. Land ownership within the Malpai Borderlands Group.

the effect, intended or not, of cultivating trust and friendships which became indispensable factors in the group's success when it turned later from discussion to action. An enormous advantage lay in the fact that the participants were farsighted enough to address their concerns before they became crises.

The role of The Nature Conservancy (TNC) proved to be essential in helping move the group from being a forum for discussion into an action organization. The Conservancy had been the area's largest landowner, having purchased

local ranching family who purchased it with a conservation easement attached, which guaranteed that the Gray would never be developed. The relationship that developed between the family and Conservancy personnel led to their inclusion in Malpai Group discussion sessions. TNC brought organizational skills, fundraising expertise, legal know-how, and additional contacts in the political world and in the scientific community. To some, however, there was a downside. Some ranchers feared the direct involvement of an international environmental group in a grassroots organization, believing the Conservancy would inevitably take over control. A few ranchers disengaged from the group, and some went so far as to begin a campaign of opposition.

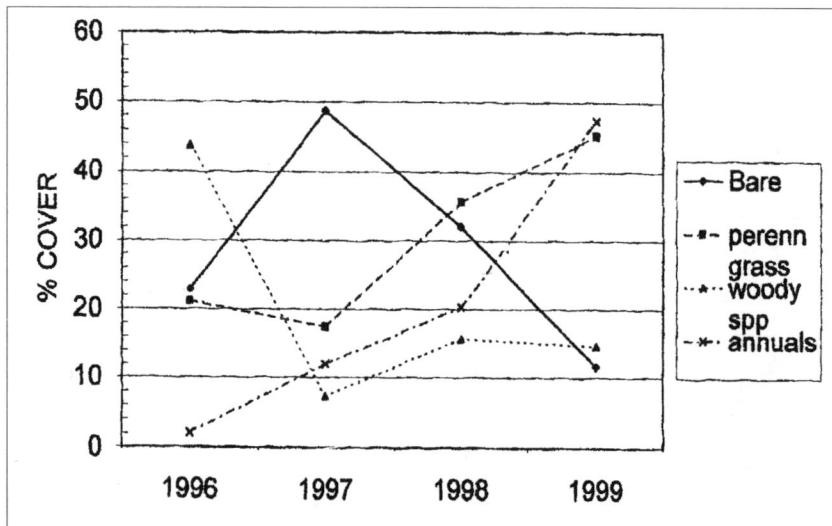

Figure 3. Monitoring results after prescribed burns.

land. The timing was fortuitous. With a mandate for ecosystem management coming from Washington, and no one exactly sure what it meant, some of the progressive minds in the agencies saw this as an opportunity to define it "on the ground."

In 1994, the Malpai Borderlands Group (MBG) was born as a nonprofit organization, establishing official status in order to receive tax-deductible contributions and hold conservation easements. A board of directors was established, made up initially of the remaining participants from the Malpai discussion group. The Forest Service and the Natural Resources Conservation Service each assigned individuals to work with the fledgling organization. An additional boost came when a multi-year grant was awarded to the research arm of the Forest Service to do long-term fire and watershed studies in coordination with the group's efforts.

## Challenge

One huge challenge for the group was trying to involve the Bureau of Land Management, the Forest Service, and two State Land Departments (altogether, owners of nearly 50 percent of the area's land) as true partners in an effort to realize an open space future for the 800,000-acre landscape (Figure 2). The Malpai Group addressed this issue by rallying the agencies around the idea of a regional fire management plan, which would include private landowner input. Agency personnel showed enthusiasm for the initiative and encouraged expansion of the idea to a whole ecosystem approach to management of the area's

## Shared Success

In addition to many tours and meetings with key officials and occasional trips to Washington, D.C., one of the things that has made the partnership with the agencies work has been the shared success in achieving stated goals. All parties (agencies, ranchers, scientists, and the environmental community) agreed that fire needed reintroduction into the landscape. The timing was right as 1994 proved to be a big year for natural fires. Because of our working relationship with the agencies, over 100,000 acres were allowed to burn. Successful prescribed burns were carried out. The Baker Burn in 1995, the Maverick Burn in 1997, and the Miller Burn in 1998 all involved multi-agency and multi-landowner cooperative efforts. The prescribed burns allowed the use of "before and after" monitoring to document whether the results met expectations (Figure 3). Did the hoped-for impact on woody species occur? Was the grass invigorated? Is the anticipated increase in biodiversity taking place? Over 200 monitoring plots are now in place in the region, many measuring fire effects.

Different challenges presented themselves depending on the land ownership involved in the burns. For prescribed burns on state and privately owned land, the biggest concern was being able to obtain the resources to actually implement a burn and ensure that the fire did not spread to places where it wasn't wanted. On federal land, abundant resources are available, but planning costs and delays resulting from different opinions on the short-term effects of fire on endangered species present (or believed to be present) made for an excruciating process leading right up to ignition. Currently, MBG is immersed in a programmatic approach to consultation on endangered species in the area. We hope this will result in a more efficient and more predictable method of implementing prescribed burns in the future.

## Endangered Species

The Malpai Borderlands Group has been proactive in rare and

> "The MBG helped initiate a Conservation Plan that became the template for the Jaguar Recovery Plan when the animal was listed as endangered in the United States.....the group maintains a fund to reimburse ranchers for any losses to livestock from a jaguar and actively funds and participates in research and monitoring efforts, ..."

endangered species issues. The group's work in helping an area ranching family with their efforts to save a threatened species of leopard frog (*Rana Chiracahuaensis*) led to a cooperative effort that included the Arizona Game and Fish Department and established a new water source on the ranch that benefits both the frogs and the family's livestock operation. Some of the tadpoles that hatch on the ranch are placed in ponds constructed at schools in nearby Douglas, Arizona as part of an education and recovery project overseen by herpetologists from the University of Arizona. Eventually, these frogs will be released back in the wild as appropriate habitats become available.

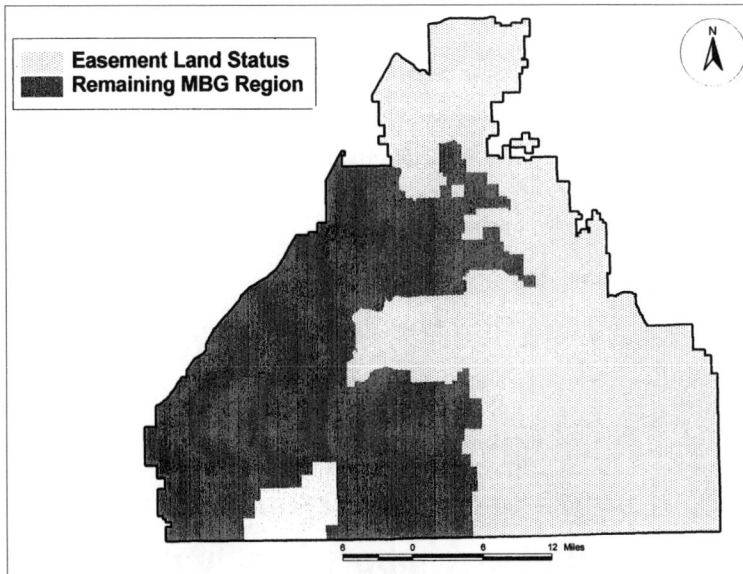

Figure 4. Easements protect about half the land area from development.

A chance encounter with a jaguar by another Malpai participant presented the group with an additional opportunity to be proactive. Instead of shooting the animal, the rancher took photographs, which were published in a booklet. The MBG helped initiate a Conservation Plan that became the template for the Jaguar Recovery Plan when the animal was listed as endangered in the United States. With the proceeds from sales of the booklet, the group maintains a fund to reimburse ranchers for any losses to livestock from a jaguar and actively funds and participates in research and monitoring efforts, most of which are conducted in Mexico.

These proactive efforts by the MBG have enhanced its credibility when it has been forced to react to court-ordered biological opinions involving federal grazing allotments in the area, which result from lawsuits being filed against the agencies. The group's ability to bring good science to bear on individual species issues has become respected in this arena, where the law requires answers to what is often unknown.

## Threat of Development

The most immediate threat to the Malpai Group's goal of securing a million acres of healthy, unfragmented landscape is the inexorable movement of people into the remaining open spaces of the West. In its attempt to keep development at bay, the group has been obtaining conservation easements on working cattle ranches in the area. Combined with the easement held by TNC on the Gray Ranch, approximately half of the land area is now permanently protected from development (Figure 4).

Conservation easements have been the biggest single factor in the recruitment of participants in the group's activities. By being flexible in anticipating and meeting the needs of ranchers, MBG has been able to provide them with more than just protection from subdivision. In exchange for the first four easements MBG received, the landowners' cattle were given multi-year access to forage on the Gray Ranch while their home ranches received needed rest from grazing following a severe drought. The Malpai Group paid for the forage by raising funds from individuals and grant-making institutions. The money is also used by the Malpai Group to work with the ranchers to share costs on the installation of watering facilities and fences, which will make the ranches more efficient and the ranchers better able to manage for droughts in the future. In two other instances, the MBG purchased the easements outright and the ranchers used the money to purchase adjoining land that will make their operations more sustainable.

In attempting to find ways to improve the economic return and provide more security to the area's ranchers, the Malpai Borderlands Group has spent considerable effort in investigating the possibility of initiating an effort to market ranch beef directly to the consumer. The idea would be to establish a premium market for quality beef from cattle raised in a beautiful, unfragmented landscape by people who were committed to keeping it that way. As appealing as that concept sounds, the reality of putting a program together in this remote area, with a limited supply of cattle (approximately 5,000 from all ranches combined), far from packing facilities, distribution centers, and urban consumers, has proved to be much more challenging than asking ranchers to work together toward conservation goals. The group is hopeful of taking some steps cooperatively to position the

ranchers' cattle to be part of a larger program, if a successful one emerges. It remains a challenge for American society to find ways to reward those who keep the land open and manage their livelihoods in an ecologically sound manner. At the least, the Malpai Group has helped to raise the visibility of the issue.

## Just Beginning

Although the Malpai Borderlands Group is being hailed as a success and a model for others, after just seven years in existence, it is clear to the group that its work is only

> "Encourage and include. Do not try to force things on people. Make opportunities available to them."

beginning and many challenges lay ahead. While the novelty of ranchers and folks from the environmental community moving away from traditional adversarial positions and working together in the "radical center" has brought the group popularity and political strength outside the region, it will be the ability of the group to stay the course over time and build on its success that will bring the eventual acceptance of those who live in the region, but have not yet participated in MBG's efforts. Nonetheless, it is apparent that the MBG has found a formula for success that has been elusive for many other similar efforts.

In conclusion, I offer a few "truisms" derived from my experience after nearly a decade of involvement with the group's efforts:

•It is important to have a written goal against which you gauge your actions and measure your success.

•Encourage and include. Do not try to force things on people. Make opportunities available to them.

•Communicate, communicate, communicate.

•Provide everyone equal access to the tools of information and analysis.

•Teach and learn. There is ample opportunity to do both.

•Obtain and use the best science available.

•Don't start what you can't finish.

•Be aware that people work hardest when it is in their best interest to do so. They work hardest together when it is in their mutual best interest.

The Gray Ranch.
(Photo courtesy of
Courtney White.)

# Marketing Conservation Value

*by Jim Winder*

Jim Winder is the owner and manager of Beck Land and Cattle Company, which operates three ranches in Nutt, Lake Valley, and Corona, New Mexico. Jim is a co-founder of The Quivira Coalition and the founder of the Heritage Ranch Foundation. The ranch at Nutt has been in Jim's family for four generations. Fifteen years ago, Jim launched a rotational grazing system in which he moves his cows every one to three days throughout the growing season. Moves are planned so that no pasture is grazed at the same time from one year to next. The range has responded dramatically. Jim has won numerous awards for his ranch management and has lectured widely on the benefits of progressive stewardship.

Lake Valley, New Mexico, was once a frontier mining town that owes its name to a series of shallow lakes fed by Berrenda Creek. In the early years of the 20th century, the lakes were drained and put into farmland. This happened because, at that time, the citizens of the United States valued the natural resources for their commodity value, and nothing more. The only way for humans to extract value from the resource was either by farming, grazing, or mining, all of which were profitable.

But times change, as do values. Today, Lake Valley is a ghost town. Once the silver played out, folks just packed up and left. And the lakes? Well, today they are being taken out of farming and put back into wetlands. Why? Because the well-fed citizens of the United States value the wetland resource more for the production of rare birds and clean water than for another bushel of corn.

It is no great secret that ranching is a mature industry and that ranchers are hard pressed to stay in business. It stands to reason that ranchers who wish to stay on the land must not be solely reliant on livestock production—they must also be able to successfully market products and services that are based on more lucrative resource values such as recreation and conservation. Although recreation is pervasive, the value of conservation is less well defined. The purpose of this article is to better understand conservation value and to lend some insights into the marketing of conservation products and services. For a rancher, this means new opportunities to make a living from the land. For the conservationist and agency employee, it offers a whole suite of powerful tools for restoration and remediation.

### Origins of Conservation Value

Back in the 1940s when recreation value first made an appear-

> "The most important job of the resource manager is to define and deliver products and services to customers which have measurable benefits for species and landscapes."

ance on the ranchlands of New Mexico, it was poorly defined and was mostly limited to services. A person might hire a rancher to take him hunting or for a mule ride up a mountain so that he could ski down. Gradually, the services became more defined and refined, and we began to see people dedicated to these services on a full-time basis. Next came the products. No self-respecting Texan would be caught dead without the newest in rifles or flannel long johns. Today, the plethora of products in a sporting goods store is testament to how well recreation value is now defined.

The conservation value of natural resources is much younger than commodities or recreation, making its appearance in the late

1960s with the widespread concern about the condition and longevity of our natural resources. When a value is new, it is usually administered by the government until the private sector takes over and begins to efficiently market the goods and services. In the early years, it was common to hear that the Environmental Protection Agency (EPA) was suing someone because of a perceived damage to a natural resource. The EPA was demonstrating our society's values by holding private companies accountable for damage done to public goods, namely air and water. Court- and agency-mandated clean-ups were often performed by contractors who benefitted financially from the environmental laws. As the private sector was forced to internalize the cost of pollution, we came to understand that it was cheaper not to pollute in the first place. Thus another industry was born, one specializing in pollution control and prevention.

The next step came as the agencies discovered that it was not enough to stop pollution, that attention needed to be focused on healing the damage that had occurred. Our society valued certain species, deemed threatened and endangered, to such a degree that billions of dollars were spent on the recovery of their populations and habitat. The key phrase here is "billions of dollars."

### The Business of Conservation

It is readily apparent that the

government and citizens of the United States value endangered species and landscapes significantly. It is also apparent that conservation has become a growth sector worth many billions of dollars annually. Now, where does this put the resource manager who is trying to make a living from the land? The most important job of the resource manager is to define and deliver to customers products and services that have measurable benefits for species and landscapes. To do this, we must understand our potential customers.

*Defining the Customer.* The first step in marketing is to define who your customers are and to understand their wants and needs. Typically, conservation customers are few in numbers but large in size. They include:

•federal, state and local governments and agencies;
•conservation groups;
•land owners.

## Government

It is important to remember that the government is the representative of the individual citizen. You should consider how your actions will benefit the voters in a specific district as well as how they will affect a specific agency. Budget cuts and environmental lawsuits have overwhelmed land management agencies like the Bureau of Land Management. The agencies are very receptive to ideas that will reduce their work load or make them less vulnerable to legal action. Agencies are organiza-

tions of people who are not rewarded for taking chances but are punished for making mistakes. Most every employee is in his/her job because they hoped to help the land. However, in a bureaucracy, it is hard for an individual to have a direct impact. When approaching an agency employee with a proposal, you should answer two questions: "How are you going protect them if something goes wrong?" "What are their personal goals for this particular resource?"

## Conservation Groups

Few ranchers have an accurate understanding of the structure and function of conservation groups, such as The Nature Conservancy or the Sierra Club. These groups are not the environmental machines they are made out to be. Instead they are simply organizations made up of people who face the same problems as other organizations. Their most important jobs are public relations and convincing people to give them money, for without PR there is no money, and without money there is no power. Large conservation groups have a bureaucracy of their own, the perpetuation of which is a higher priority than the resolution of resource conflicts. When dealing with a group, you should consider first what is good for the group and secondly what is good for the land.

## Land Owners

Increasingly there is a separation between who owns the land and who manages the land. Large trophy ranches are being purchased by folks who haven't a clue as to which end of the cow gets up first. Most ranch managers understand cows and grass but often fail to understand the true goals and values of the property owner. The owner did not buy the ranch because of the great financial rewards it offered. Instead it was purchased to fulfill certain emotional rewards which come from owning a tract of land. An astute manager recognizes this and manages the resource to improve wildlife populations, riparian habitat, and scenic beauty. This may sound esoteric, but it is well founded in economics. After all, the owner will probably sell the ranch to another person with similar values and more wildlife, creeks, and beauty will be reflected in the increased sales price of the land.

*Defining Products and Services.* In order for your product or service to be economically successful, it has to deliver a benefit to the customer. It is important to remember that a benefit can be either the addition of something positive or the removal of something negative. A good rule of thumb is that the more conflict there is involving a resource, the more opportunity there is for profit. Potential products and services may be found under one of the following broad categories:

•species recovery;

•scenic beauty and open space;

•clean air and water;

•control of exotic and invading species;

•preservation of resources for future generations.

As you define your products and services, it is useful to ask two questions: "What good things can I produce?" "What bad things can I make disappear?" Let's examine each of the above categories in turn and see what opportunities they hold.

## Species Recovery

There is little doubt that our society values threatened and endangered species. Although some species, such as the Bald Eagle, may have more public appeal than a less charismatic species, such as a snail, most scientists refuse to place relative importance on any species, stating that each species deserves protection in its own right. However, few would argue that it is easier to raise funds and to attract attention for the more charismatic species. Often, the value of a species is based on potential future uses such as medicine, and on their ecological functions. Clearly, many species perform functions that would be uneconomical for man to replace. Think of the role that grasses play in the production of clean water from our watersheds, and what it would cost to replace them with some manmade structure, if it were possible at all.

Now we ask our two little questions: "What good thing can I produce that will help this species? Is there something missing that we can provide—new habitat, a research facility or even improved landowner cooperation?" Secondly: "What bad things can I make go away?" Endangered species are endangered for a reason. A little research will often reveal what the experts consider to be the cause of the species' decline and the factors that limit recovery. Often, a combination of several factors such as loss of habitat or competition from other species is to blame. Almost always, there is a human policy constraint involved as well. What can you do to remove a key constraint?

## Scenic Beauty and Open Space

I once participated in a panel discussion with a professor of economics from the University of Montana. The professor used a variety of slides and overheads to demonstrate to the audience that there was an economic boom occurring in the western states. He also effectively demonstrated that this boom was not due to livestock, mining, or logging. So what was driving the boom? It was people retiring to the West to live in a beautiful place and the money they brought with them. In addition, many high-tech companies were locating in mountain cities in order to provide a higher quality of life for their employees.

The next thing this learned professor demonstrated was that land with nice views carried a significantly higher value than places less well endowed. This held for the grand views of a mountain range as well as for more local views of things like a healthy stream. It stands to reason that a creek lined with green grass and trees is worth more than one with barren banks and stagnant water.

There are many ways to make a landscape less visually appealing—construction of roads, buildings, fences, and power lines are just a few. Cowpies in the campgrounds and hammered riparian areas are common complaints on public lands. When we get beyond seeing only cows and grass, we can then find alternatives which meet our needs but which do not have a negative visual impact. Society also values the open space on a ranch. It may be profitable to fill your valley with houses; then again, it can be profitable to leave it open. Development rights can be sold and retired for real cash money. If nothing else, a tax write-off is always available.

## Clean Air and Water

For a product to have economic value, it must be scarce. For a long time, clean air and water were not considered to have economic value because of their abundance. When the world was less populated with humans, we could pollute and move away and nature would clean up our mess. Then came our massive, sedentary populations which could easily overwhelm nature's ability to break down our waste. The air became brown and the rivers caught fire.

Although our air and water are cleaner than in the past, we are still faced with declining and over-allocated water supplies in the West. Spend a winter morning in Albuquerque and you see there is still

Jim [left] giving a tour of his riparian area. (Photo courtesy of Courtney White.)

much room to improve our air.

Clean air and water are hands down the most valuable products of our rangelands, but they have been the hardest to get paid for. This is changing. It is widely recognized that an acre of grassland can absorb more carbon from the atmosphere than an acre of rainforest. It is also recognized that plowed fields give off carbon into the atmosphere. We are beginning to see these facts make their way into the government psyche in the form of carbon credits. The creation of a market for pollution credits has been heralded by economists as the most effective way to control pollution. (Environmentalists take a dimmer view of the system.) Under this system, a factory is allowed to

pollute to a certain point. If their pollution is less, then they are given credits. These credits can be sold to other factories that are less able to reduce their pollution. The results are that the efficient factories reduce more pollution and at a lower cost than the less efficient factories and are rewarded for their efforts.

Municipalities are faced with the large cost of providing clean water for their citizens. Pollution comes in many forms, including soil sediments. Municipalities have begun to purchase surrounding ranches to protect their watershed and reduce water treatment costs. The door is open for resource managers who can provide the watershed protection at a lower cost while producing other valuable goods such as livestock.

## Control of Exotic Species

A variety of exotic species have been accidentally or purposely introduced into native rangelands with disastrous local results. Leafy spurge, Zebra mussels, and dozens of other exotic species have become a type of living pollution. State, federal, and local governments have dumped millions of dollars worth of chemicals on the land in an effort to control noxious plants. But often these same plants can be controlled through grazing with sheep and goats. The economics of a livestock operation are greatly improved when the forage is free—now think how good they can be when you get paid to graze. This approach is also applicable to the control of native weeds under power line rights-of-way. The point is to see livestock as tools. A sheep is much cheaper to operate than a bulldozer.

### Preservation of Resources for Future Generations

Sometimes we are not able to find a way to market the value from certain resources, but we can still get paid for doing nothing. Our society values the preservation of natural resources for future generations. Not only do they need resources to survive, it is highly probable that our children and grandchildren will have a better understanding of natural resources than we have today. Also their values will be different than ours.

There exist a variety of government programs that help resource managers improve the resource without demanding a short-term profit. Other programs actually purchase certain rights which are deemed to be hazardous to the future resource uses. Mining, drilling, and development rights may be sold for cash or donated and a tax write-off taken.

### Getting Paid

The markets in agriculture are so well defined and developed that a rancher can sell a cow any number of ways, any day of the week. The conservation market is not

yet to this point. Herein lies the opportunity. Although direct cash payments for conservation work are available, often the payment takes other forms. Resource improvements that are paid for by the government or conservation groups make the resource more productive and allow

> "It is widely recognized that an acre of grassland can absorb more carbon from the atmosphere than an acre of rainforest."

indirect profits. An example of this is a wetland improvement project. Although the money received may be strictly allocated to moving dirt to improve the wetland, people will pay to come and view the wildlife that are attracted to the water.

Another method is to wrap a non-conservation product in conservation. An example is predator-friendly wool products, which differentiates a commodity by its impact on the resource. Or bird watching, which winds conservation around a recreational experience.

Finally, given the public's preconception that conservation is best performed by governments or non-profit groups, many of the payments for conservation work are made through grants. There are literally hundreds of sources for conservation grants in the United States. Federal agencies from Interior to Defense offer conservation-oriented grants. State agencies and private foundations are some additional, more local sources.

The West Elk Wilderness, which is grazed. (Photo courtesy of Courtney White.)

## Conclusions

The conservation of natural resources is a new value which offers resource managers an improved opportunity for profits. Like any new and developing industry, conservation rewards the person who has the vision to recognize an opportunity among conflict. In fact, the greater the conflict, the greater the potential rewards are for someone holding a solution. Up to now, much of the conservation activities were directly controlled by government or large conservation groups. Because of their size and detachment from the resource, these entities are not efficient. Thus an opportunity exists for those people who can accomplish a conservation task at a lower cost. No one is in a position to know the resource better than the person who lives on

the land. However, often, a rancher will fail to understand business opportunities that exist on his land merely because it requires work that is different than what his daddy did.

This article was not intended to be a cookbook approach to marketing conservation. Instead, it was written to open the reader's mind just a little and hopefully show a few ranchers that there is a whole new world out there. Let your neighbor spend his money on genetics and hormones. If you are serious about keeping your family on the land, then you need to be serious about growing beyond ranching to be a resource manager. The ranching industry is at one of the most critical crossroads of its history. Does it stick with tradition and continue its disappearing act? Or does it recognize that it is in the resource management business and prosper by producing the goods and services the public demands?

The conservationist or agency employee should recognize the benefits of managing endangered resources through the capitalist system. Economics is a subset of ecology, and there is no more efficient way of managing natural resources towards the public's goals. It was once profitable to destroy ecosystems, now it can be profitable to restore them.

An Invitation to the Radical Center

# Dry Times: Managing Through a Drought
*by Kirk L. Gadzia*

**K**irk Gadzia works with ranchers across the United States and internationally to improve the sustainability of their operations. The foundation of Kirk's approach is that profitable ranching isn't about harder work; it is about making better decisions. In looking at each business as a whole, his work involves financial planning, grazing management, wildlife interactions, improving land health, and management-training courses on a public and private basis. Kirk has more than 20 years experience in working on rangeland-health issues. He is co-author of *Rangeland Health* (National Academy of Sciences, 1994), and he has developed and implemented range-monitoring techniques to provide early-warning indicators of deteriorating rangeland health. Kirk has a B.S. in Wildlife Biology and an M.S. in Range Science.

If only it would rain! These words have been heard in many parts of the West this year and echoed through the centuries as agriculturists looked to the skies for salvation from drought. While more rain would certainly help the current situation, there is little more that we can do, except to wish, to actually cause more rain to fall.

Unfortunately, it seems that many ranchers caught in the current drought cycle will use "wishing it would rain" as their main tactic for survival. But hope alone will only ensure that the important steps you should take now to manage your ranch and business most effectively will be put off until it is too late to act. The key components of managing through a drought mirror the whole that encompasses any ranching operation. Namely: people, money, and land. This article will examine ways you can actively affect your future and that of the ranch in a drought cycle.

## People-Centered Principles

The single greatest aspect of managing through a drought is the attitude of the persons who are in charge and making decisions. Franklin D. Roosevelt once said, "The only thing we have to fear is fear itself." Fear is a natural reaction when you feel out of control of any situation that is critical to your security. While fear may be a good motivator, it often creates the climate for poor decision making. The key to overcoming this is to gain mental control over the situation. This requires that you make a plan of how your plan to paper if you want it to succeed. For example, if you plan to destock, when do you plan to do so? How many animals and which individuals or classes of stock are you planning on taking action on? When these factors are put on paper, the consequences, in terms of money, forage savings, etc., can be clearly evaluated.

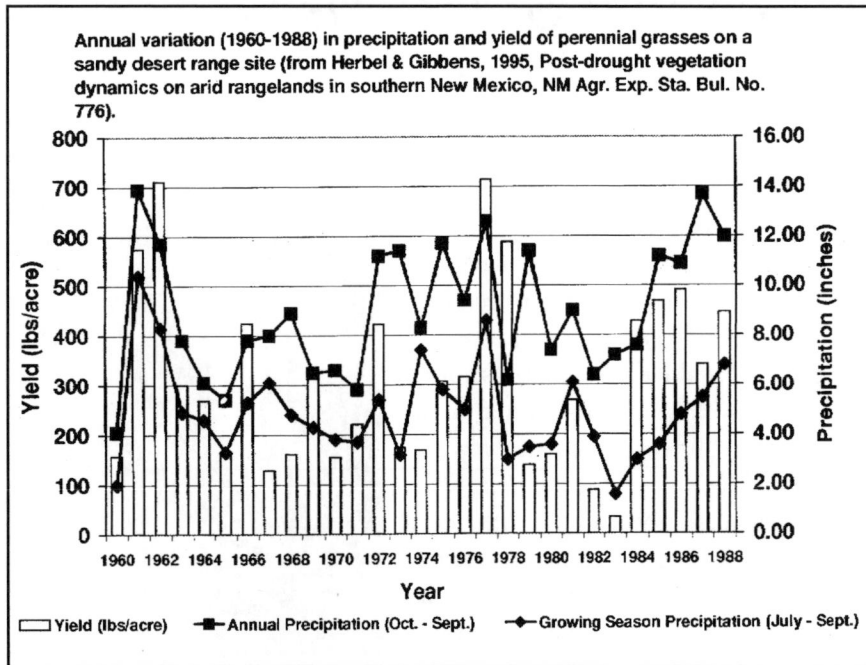

Figure 1. Annual variation in precipitation and grass yield, 1960-1988.

you are going to deal with the drought and take action on your plan.

However, skipping the planning aspect of this strategy is all too common. It reminds me of the accuracy we are likely to achieve if we follow the orders, "Ready, Fire, Aim!" Once you commit to taking an active rather than a passive role in drought management, the planning or aiming must be done first.

Ask yourself if you have a written drought plan in place, or must you create one now? Most people would answer that they have a plan, but it is not written down. There is in fact a big difference between a rough mental idea and a clearly laid out plan that you and others can see and discuss. Commit

Remember that the drought you are now experiencing is a normal part of the weather pattern (Figure 1). In fact, climate data indicate that much of the West has experienced a long-term wet cycle and that we are overdue for drier conditions to return (Figure 2). While this offers little encouragement, take the long-term view that what you learn by managing your way through this tough time will help you even more the next time drought occurs.

Doing the hard work of initial evaluation and planning will also highlight the strategic or long-term factors you should have been taking action on while times were relatively good. Although you may be constrained from doing so now, make sure items such as water development, cross fencing, or other methods of gaining control of the timing, intensity, and frequency of grazing become a high priority when you are contemplating future actions and expenditures.

Planning is difficult to do on your own. Now is the time to reach out to co-workers, friends, and others for creative ideas and help in evaluating your written strategy. Seek out and work with those who have a

## Financial-Centered Principles

The link between human and financial principles in drought management is very strong. Three human tendencies often keep us from creating a profitable plan:

—The tendency to allow production costs to rise to anticipated income.

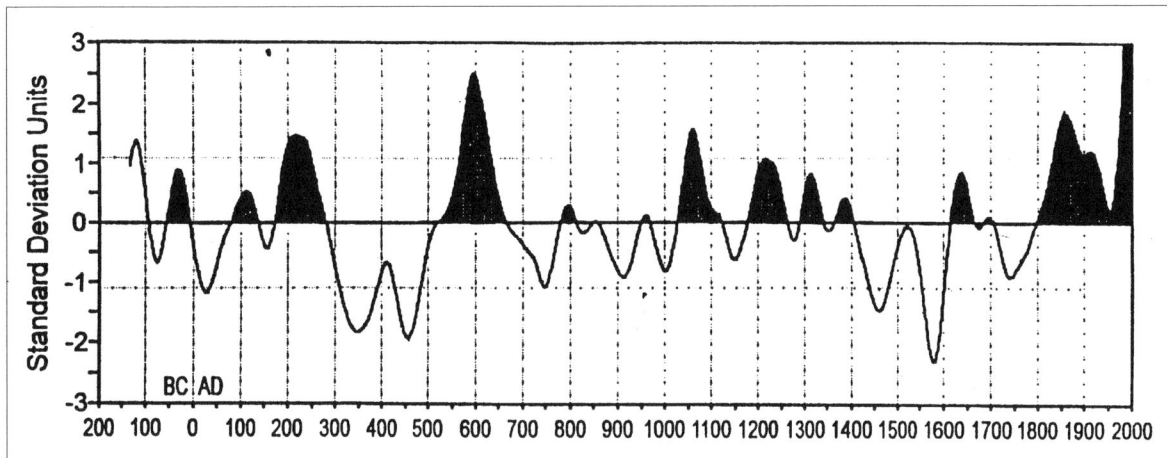

positive attitude. Don't spend your time at the local "gloom and doom" café with those who will just reinforce the fact that times are tough.

The truth is that most people will avoid the hard work and office time of planning that could actually help them survive a tough situation such as a drought. They seem paralyzed by the conflicting emotions of fear and hope that the drought triggers. Meanwhile, local prices plummet for the commodities they cling to, their land and long-term productivity deteriorates from poor management decisions, and they often end up spending money they can never hope to recoup.

—The tendency to borrow against anticipated income.

—The tendency to spend very little time or effort planning on paper. Monitoring efforts are often too late or non-existent.

Planning for a profit is different than budgeting or cash flowing. It is about aggressively setting a target level for income and expenses and having the management determination to bring your plan to fruition.

You are unlikely to make sound financial decisions if you have not committed to maintaining a positive, "take charge" attitude in the face of adversity. Likewise, the written drought plan you produce

Figure 2. July-July precipitation for the period 136 BC to AD 1992 reconstructed from the MLC, converted to standard deviation units, and represented as a 100-year smoothing spline. The 100-year spline emphasizes long-term (100 years) trends in past precipitation.

will obviously have financial conse-quences for each option you con-sider. You must work through several scenarios to determine the best

---

**Financial-Centered Principles**

Get in charge of your financial situation and have a plan for profit.

Build cash reserves from good years to help you through lean times.

Have a stock reduction plan and know the financial consequences of all proposed actions in advance.

Water developments and fencing are cheaper investments than drought feed, and they keep paying dividends for long periods of time.

Replan your livestock production and annual financial plan to reflect proposed actions. Keep your banker and tax advisor informed of your decisions.

Marketing is still possible, even in a drought. Are you letting others profit from your situation by avoiding marketing and other options?

Remember that drought feeding is seldom a good investment.

Do the paperwork and make the calculations yourself.

---

course of action for your particular situation. For example, what will destocking cost you this year, and in coming years, if breeding stock are sold? How does destocking by 10% early in the season compare with having to destock by 50% late in the season if no significant rainfall occurs?

Knowing these numbers means you can choose the best course of action compatible with the risk that your business and you can bear. It also means that you can keep your banker, tax advisor, and business partners informed in a timely man-ner of the likely financial conse-quences of the drought. Few people appreciate financially disastrous surprises, least of all bankers. Re-plan your livestock production worksheets and annual financial plan to reflect proposed actions and consequences. Enlist the help of your financial advisors and partners in finding solutions to any shortfalls and deciding the most appropriate actions.

Since profitability may be a difficult goal in a drought, you must plan some reserves that are generated in good years to help you through the lean times. These may be in-vested in the business as easily liquidated assets or kept as interest-generating reserves. If you have never done so before, put a plan for building reserves into action when the drought breaks.

Just like reserves, many of the suggested financial principles require action prior to a drought to be effective. Investments in long-term water availability and alternative control of animal movements such as fencing or herding allow you greater flexibility in planning your grazing to minimize the effects of drought and the need for massive destocking. Have you made the investments in your own training to explore alterna-tive grazing strategies and manage-ment methods? These kinds of investments are cheaper than drought feeding and keep paying dividends for long periods of time.

The low prices that develop regionally in drought-stricken areas provide a double whammy to live-stock producers who must destock.

Remember that marketing is still possible in a drought. Are you letting others profit from your situation by avoiding marketing? Another related benefit to planning early destocking by smaller amounts is that you tend to get a higher price for those animals you do sell.

A ranching friend in Colorado recently told me about a neighbor of his who was feeding a group of cows in adverse conditions. When he stopped to talk to him, the neighbor remarked that, "With this high-priced hay, I've already got more money tied up in these cows than their calves can hope to bring this fall." My friend then asked his neighbor what he was going to do. The reply was, "I guess I'll feed 'em."

Purchasing feed is a common reaction during a drought. It usually has financially disastrous consequences due to the fact that, unless the feed is extremely cheap and locally available, you are unlikely to ever regain the value of any feeding program. The "hope" is that the feeding will only have to take place for a short while, "just until we get some rain." Unfortunately, you do not have a clue as to how long the drought will persist, and you are likely to exhaust your financial resources on this expensive delaying tactic.

---

**Principles for Land and Livestock**

Do your dormant season planning! Assume no more forage will grow. Determine how much existing forage there is and how long it will last with current numbers or various stock reduction options.

Become accurate at estimating Animal Days per Acre (ADAs) of forage on the land in various conditions.

Combine herds as soon as possible. Combining herds gives you more flexibility and reduces grazing periods relative to recovery periods.

Increase recovery periods for pastures as long as possible.

Be creative about increasing pasture numbers per herd. Use temporary fencing and work with others to combine herds and increase numbers of pastures available.

Plan long-term water availability and volume. Put your plan into action when times are good.

Remember that drought effects are less severe when the water cycle is functioning effectively. Plan your grazing carefully at all times.

Be prepared to vary stock numbers according to a stock reduction plan.

Reduce numbers early, according to predetermined critical dates. Prices will be better, and there will be more feed for the remaining stock.

For breeding herds, wean offspring early. Consider options such as delayed breeding and/or reduced breeding vs. selling your genetics.

Remember that drought feeding is rarely a good investment. Calculate the costs and make the comparisons yourself.

Ensure your enterprise mix is compatible with drought risk in your area.

---

## Principles for Land and Livestock

Many of the principles put forward for human and financial management during a drought also apply to the land and livestock. Mental preparation for tough decisions is the first step. Creating a plan for dealing with your actions in a well-thought-out manner is second. Understanding how the land reacts to drought and your options for livestock management are the third.

Water cycle refers to the effectiveness of capturing, storing, and safely releasing rainfall. Rangeland can have an effective or non-

An example of an area on Sandia Pueblo with a poor water cycle. (Photo courtesy of Kirk Gadzia.)

effective water cycle depending on how we manage. If the water cycle is effective, the land will be well covered with plants and plant material so that water is captured and incorporated into soil where it falls. Conversely, an ineffective water cycle on the same area will be characterized by low plant densities and lack of soil cover, leading to high runoff and evaporation rates.

The difference in response of such areas to limited rainfall is dramatic. An inch of rainfall in an area with an effective water cycle can produce double or triple the forage amounts that it can where the cycle is ineffective. This factor alone can mean the difference between financial ruin or sustainability in a ranching situation.

The single biggest influence

on rainfall effectiveness on land grazed by livestock is the manner in which the livestock are managed. If grazed plants are given adequate recovery periods to restore the removed plant parts and underground root systems, this enhances the effectiveness of the water cycle. In addition, limiting the exposure time of the animals to the plants and soil also tends to improve the water cycle through reduced compaction. Overgrazing of plants (prolonged grazing periods and inadequate recovery periods) tends to shorten root systems underground, which makes them even more sensitive to drought.

Having a better understanding of the water cycle is crucial to managing in a drought. You cannot create an effective water cycle overnight. It must be cultivated through careful management over the years and through wet and dry cycles. Thus, planning grazing carefully even when times are good is just as important as doing so in a drought. Research also shows that areas with effective water cycles recover much more quickly from a drought.

The most important factor in grazing management during a drought is to increase the recovery periods given to an area that is grazed. Increasing recovery periods without excessively prolonging grazing periods requires that you have more pastures per herd. This can be practically accomplished by combining herds, working with neighbors, constructing temporary fences, herding, or other creative ways of keeping the animals moving onto fresh ground and letting areas where they have grazed recover longer. Remember, these will be options only if watering facilities are adequate.

useable forage is a common method employed by many agencies and some ranchers. This can be translated into Animal Unit Months (AUMs) of forage available and compared with the AUMs of forage you are planning to remove. Perhaps

The plan for the livestock will probably need to include a stock reduction aspect.

In order to make this decision with some degree of accuracy, you must be able to inventory your forage resources as soon as drought conditions warrant. When doing this, you should normally assume that what forage is present is all that there will be. You now need to know how much that is, and how long it will last with the stock you have on hand and with various stock reduction options you may be considering. Wildlife also make their home on most ranches, and you will need to make cover and feed allowances for their survival as well.

There are many ways of assessing forage quantity on land. Estimating pounds per acre of

a more user-friendly method is to estimate the Animal Days per Acre (ADAs) of forage remaining. This is a relatively simple way of calculating forage based on visual samples of the land in various areas. It is rapid, easy to learn, and can be very accurate with practice.

Stock reduction is a difficult decision to make. Your plan should indicate which groups of animals will be sold first and by what date. Again, remember that the earlier you make the decision to reduce, the more likely you are to get a better price and the more feed will remain for the stock that are not sold. You do run the risk of selling too early and then getting rainfall. But weigh this against the risk of delaying the decision and the drought continuing. You will then have to destock signifi-

Where vegetation is dense, water flows are tortuous. Erosive energy is dissipated, and more water absorbs into the ground as it moves across the land. (Source: Ludwig *et al.* 1997:15, *Landscape Ecology, Function and Management: Principles from Australia's Rangelands.*)

cantly more head, and the animals you sell are likely to be in poorer condition and bring a lower price.

Other options for breeding livestock are to wean the calves early and sell them. A dry animal is much better able to maintain itself in tough conditions. Depending on your enterprises, you may also consider delayed breeding or only exposing a portion of the stock. This might be an option when you have very valuable genetics and selling females is worse than not having offspring to sell. Obviously each of these decisions has financial consequences that should be calculated and put in your plan.

Drought-prone areas should always include a large margin of safety in dormant season biological plans. This is referred to as a "drought reserve," and in some areas should amount to almost a full year of forage. If you are in an area that typically has highly erratic rainfall patterns, consider your enterprise mix carefully. The most difficult enterprise to deal with when destocking must be done is the cow-calf enterprise. Stocker enterprises

and small stock such as sheep and goats are more adapted to the fluctuations that may be needed in a drought. Running a mix of enterprises may be a good choice in such areas.

## Summary

The key to surviving a drought is planning the consequences to land, people, money, and animals as a whole. The tradition of hoping it will rain and then taking expensive reactionary steps when it does not has proven disastrous. What is needed is a plan for action based on calculations of forage availability, financial consequences of various options, and the implementation of progressive management that will improve the long-term resilience of the land and business.

(Photo courtesy of Courtney White.)

---

**People-Centered Principles**

FDR said, "We have nothing to fear but fear itself." Attitude is everything!

You must be in charge of the situation rather than reacting to circumstances.

Make a drought plan, and be prepared to make difficult strategic and financial decisions.

Accept the fact that paperwork and planning will do more to help during the drought than worrying and spending money. Don't fear the office and the computer.

Accept the fact that droughts are a normal part of ranching and that what you learn from the current drought will help you through the next one.

Work with others who have a positive attitude and spend less time at the coffee shop!

---

# The Southwestern Willow Flycatcher and Me

*by David Ogilvie*

D avid Ogilvie is the owner-manager of the Ogilvie Cattle Company and the manager of U Bar Ranch. David and his wife Tammy moved their family from Arizona in 1985 to the Cliff/Gila Valley. Since then, David has practiced rest/rotation grazing on his ranch and on the U Bar. He says, "Since moving here, I've discovered the Cliff/Gila Valley is unique in many ways. The diversity of wildlife in the area is amazing." David has worked to manage the U Bar in such a way as to both protect and enhance its population of the endangered Southwestern Willow Flycatcher, as well as the other populations of migratory birds.

U Bar Ranch is a commercial ranching and farming operation in southwestern New Mexico along the Gila River. The ranch can be considered an environmental paradox because the largest known and most successful population of Southwestern Willow Flycatchers is found on the private land that we graze and farm.

Seldom a day goes by that one does not read in some publication or hear over some broadcast media of the endangerment of this species. Most environmental groups, with few exceptions, are calling for the removal of all livestock along riparian or riverine systems as the solution. The accusation is that livestock grazing (cattle in particular) have led the Flycatcher to the brink of extinction.

## *Federal Register* Targets Livestock

One would only have to go to the listing of the Proposed Rules in the *Federal Register* of July 23, 1993 to find extensive references to the so-called negative influence caused by agriculture or livestock grazing. The many factors listed by the publication include destruction and overuse by livestock, cowbird parasitism, modification to the habitat resulting in invasions of exotic tamarisk or other non-native species, water diversion and impoundment, channelization of rivers and so on. In reading the listing, one finds that agriculture (specifically, cattle grazing) is identified as the cause of the demise of this song bird. If one was to believe all the information regarding this species' endangered status, you would immediately

---

assume that the factors cited in the *Register* would have been scientifically studied, based, and supported. But, are they?

Southwestern Willow Flycatcher Breeding Sites

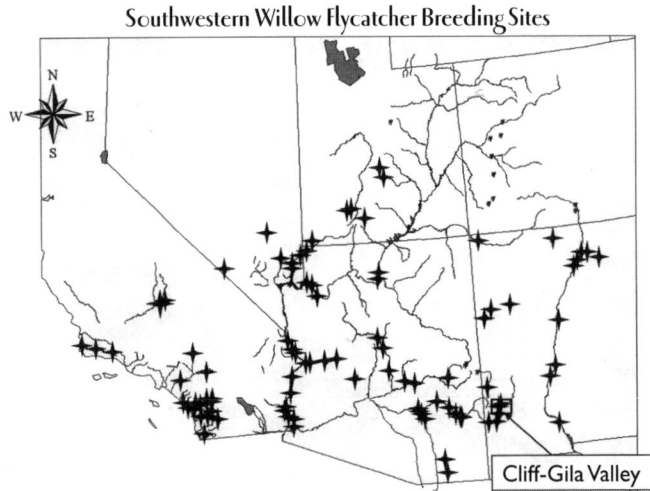

Figure 1. Range of the Southwestern Willow Flycatcher. Crosses indicate known breeding sites. Approximately 930 territories are distributed among 209 sites, according to the most recent estimates (U.S. Fish and Wildlife Service 2001).

U Bar Ranch's involvement with the Flycatcher began with the *Federal Register's* listing because it referenced the Gila River. A total of 643 miles of stream and river were proposed as habitat, including the entire Gila River system.

## Population Survey

U Bar Ranch's concern was that we knew very little about the Southwestern Willow Flycatcher and wanted information regarding its status on the private land we lease. In response to our concerns, a population survey of the birds inhabiting the U Bar was undertaken in May 1994 by qualified biologists using an established U.S. Fish & Wildlife Service protocol. The population survey continued through June and ended in July 1994, showing a high population of 64 pairs. It

should be noted that, in 1997, the second largest population known was located on the Kern River in California, with 38 pairs. U Bar Ranch's population in 1994 was almost twice that.

Another interesting observation during the initial 1994 survey year was that the nesting habitats of preference on U Bar were not young dense stands of willow and cottonwood as identified, but flood plain forest patches comprised mostly of box elder, older mature cottonwood and willow, and introduced Russian olive trees. These trees are more commonly found protected from the river in secondary stringers located along old earthen irrigation ditches. Even more interesting was that cowbird parasitism was not commonly observed.

Population surveys have been conducted every year since 1994. The 1995 survey ended with 107 pairs, the 1996 survey with 138 pairs, the 1997 survey with 174 pairs, and the 1998 survey with 186 pairs. Keep in mind that the next highest population is 38 pairs where there is no livestock. Coincidentally, with the increase of Flycatchers came a corresponding increase in farm ground that U Bar Ranch put under irrigation. In 1995, U Bar Ranch returned approximately 300 acres of fallow farm ground to irrigation production, with an additional 280 acres being returned to production in 1996.

## Research Expanded

With these interesting departures from the best available scientific information, it was felt that there was a need to expand the scope of the research. In April 1997, the Rocky Mountain Research Station of the U.S. Forest Service, headed by Dr. Scott Stoleson, was asked to be involved along with Dr. Dale Zimmerman, professor emeritus, Western New Mexico University, a respected ornithologist, and Dr. Roland Shook, also of Western New Mexico University. Credibility of the research was of prime consideration, and the issue of credibility could be addressed with the cooperation of these other parties.

Specific objectives in the expanded research included evaluating the population densities of all breeding bird species in habitat patches occupied by Willow Flycatchers, evaluating reproductive success of Willow Flycatchers, quantifying nest-site characteristics of Willow Flycatchers, and quantifying the floristic and landscape-level characteristics of occupied habitat.

With this expansion of the research, many interesting and significant observations have been made. Although the habitat found on U Bar Ranch is not typically touted as Southwestern Willow Flycatcher habitat, it appears to be optimal for the species. Nesting success is higher than in any other known population, with the lowest parasitism by cowbirds found anywhere. The nest placement with

regard to nest height and vegetation of preference is significantly different from what the established science has been suggesting. Some nest heights exceed 70 feet above ground. All of these situations have occurred with high densities of livestock. It is important to note that, while the regulating agencies are steadfast in adhering to regulations that call for the removal of all livestock from riparian areas, the science that supports those claims is not being substantiated.

## No Flycatchers Without Livestock

The only long-term scientific study of Southwestern Willow Flycatchers in conjunction with livestock has been on the U Bar Ranch. The identification of entire river systems in the Southwest as potential habitat (643 miles), including the Gila River system, was probably unwarranted. Extensive survey work has been done on the Gila River in the Gila National Forest and no Flycatchers have been found to exist in the narrow canyon bottoms in the absence of livestock,

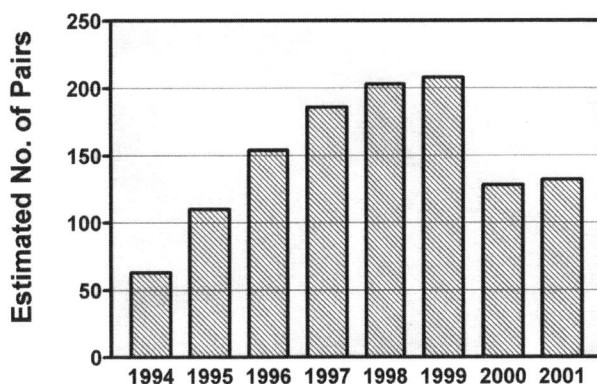

Figure 2. Population estimates for Southwestern Willow Flycatchers on the U Bar Ranch, 1994-2001. The population increased from 1994, when surveys by the Phelps Dodge consultant began, until 2000. The large drop in numbers seen that year mirrors that shown by other populations throughout the range of the Willow Flycatcher, including California, and is likely due to extended drought on the wintering grounds as far south as Costa Rica. (Figure courtesy of Dr. Scott Stoleson.)

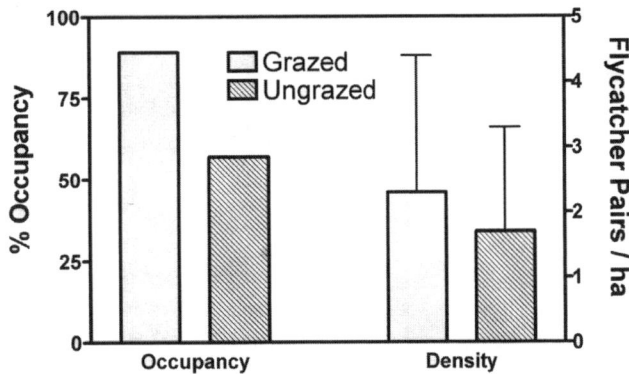

Figure 3. Comparison of rates of patch occupancy and density of flycatchers between habitat patches grazed for part of the year and patches completely excluded from grazing (ungrazed). Grazing impacted occupancy by Willow Flycatchers, although not as might be expected. While approximately half of the excluded patches had flycatchers, almost 90% of the grazed patches had flycatchers. (Figure courtesy of Dr. Scott Stoleson.)

even with excellent vegetative characteristics. Present areas with wide flood plains and older more diverse stands of flood plain forests seem to be preferred. These situations are most commonly found on private land (not public lands) used for farming or ranching.

Livestock management in riparian areas warrants special consideration. The study on U Bar Ranch demonstrates that livestock grazing can be compatible and even complementary to sustaining some habitats. One reason that the older more diverse flood plain forest patches exist in the Gila/Cliff Valley is due in part to grazing. Historically, grazing has reduced fire fuels and has provided protection from fire. Earthen farming ditches have promoted the establishment of a variety of tree species and are critical to sustaining the Flycatcher habitat. Earthen levees have allowed the floodplain forest patches to attain maturity.

### Flexible Management

U Bar Ranch's livestock management, in association with the occupied habitat, has always been flexible, with some of the pastures being grazed strictly in the dormant season, while others are used in a rest/rotation system in direct association with nesting bird activity. Most farming activities in close proximity to nesting bird habitats are minimized during the active nesting season. On U Bar Ranch, the Flycatcher population is stable and increasing even with this variety of management.

Of great concern to U Bar Ranch is the flooding activity that has occurred along the Gila River. The flooding damage is endangering occupied Flycatcher habitat. We are interested in participating in projects that protect older known habitats and encourage new habitat growth. An example of this involves a completed restoration project on the Gila National Forest with which U Bar Ranch is involved as a permittee. The techniques used to restore a flood damaged section of the river were not commonly accepted. They involved redirecting the river away from exposed vertical soil banks with gravel berms and exposing the water table below the berms to enable planting of native riparian vegetation in backwater marshes to create a vegetative barrier. The berms protected and allowed the vegetative plantings time to establish. After two or three growing seasons, they have been very successful in stabilizing the river banks. Cattle are also managed to foster the recovery of the vegetative plantings.

# An Invitation to the Radical Center

This project was started in June 1995, with additional work in 1996. Population survey work was completed in 1998 in the Gila Bird Area (the location of the project) and 8 pairs of Willow Flycatchers were found nesting where none had ever been recorded. This same area had also been extensively surveyed in previous years, starting in the 1950s, with no recorded Flycatcher sightings.

We are discouraged about the lack of support from the agencies in charge of adminstering such restoration activities. There are other sites in need of restoration in the Cliff/Gila Valley, but it has been very difficult to obtain cooperation and approval from the agencies. It is hard to understand why such agencies ignore their mandate to protect and foster populations of an endangered species with proven practices, while forcing the elimination of a valid compatible use, livestock grazing.

***Editor's Note:*** *Since this article was written (1998), further study has been conducted by Dr. Scott Stoleson. This is a summary of that research:*

The recovery and management of endangered species requires a clear understanding of both their habitat requirements and how variation in habitat might affect nesting success. The endangered Southwestern Willow Flycatcher (*Empidonax traillii extimus*), a riparian-obligate, neotropical migrant,

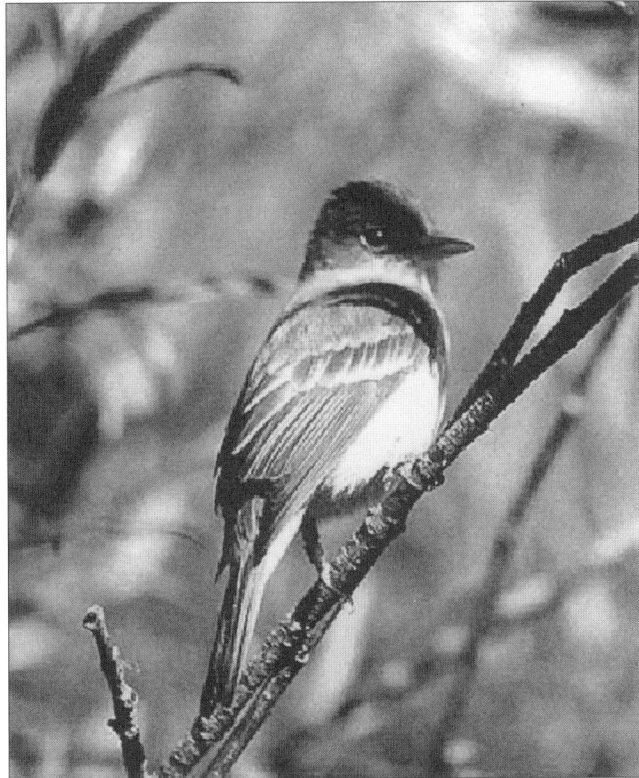

The Southwestern Willow Flycatcher.

breeds at numerous sites across the region that vary greatly in floristics, vegetation structure, and the extent of human alteration of occupied habitats. Its decline has been attributed to habitat loss from a variety of factors, including grazing.

The largest population occurs in the Gila River Valley of New Mexico, primarily on the U Bar Ranch. Since 1997, this population has been the focus of intensive research by a collaborative team from the USDA Forest Service Rocky Mountain Research Station, Western New Mexico University, Gila National Forest, U Bar Ranch, and Phelps Dodge Corporation. We have assessed habitat use at the scale of nest tree, home range, patch, and landscape. We have also monitored nesting success and brood parasitism. We compared the usage of different nest trees with their availability within occupied habitat to show that, in mature riparian woodland, flycatchers disproportionately nested in box elder, and significantly underutilized willows; other trees were used in proportion to their abundance. We compared values of 19 habitat variables between nest sites and unused

> "The study on U Bar Ranch demonstrates that livestock grazing can be compatible and even complementary to sustaining some habitats."

sites within occupied habitat. Compared to unused sites, microhabitat around Flycatcher nest sites was characterized by significantly lower ground cover; greater and less variable canopy cover; lower canopy height; higher foliage density in the sub-canopy; more heterogeneous foliage density; higher foliage height diversity; more stems of shrubs, trees, and box elder; fewer cottonwood stems; greater proximity to water; and different species of herbaceous vegetation. A logistic regression model suggests that the Flycatchers are cuing in to dense, shady box elder groves. Nesting success of Flycatchers correlates positively with nest height in this population.

We examined landscape- and patch-scale correlates of patch occupancy, density, nesting success, and

rates of cowbird parasitism on Willow Flycatchers. We estimated Flycatcher population size and nesting success in 39 discrete riparian patches from 1997 through 2000. Three variables were significant predictors of patch occupancy by Willow Flycatchers: percent of woody stems that were box elder, proximity to the nearest patch, and variation in shrub density. Only percent of box elder was a significant predictor of Flycatcher density within patches, reflecting the unique nesting preferences of this population.

Overall, 18 of the 39 study patches were grazed, primarily in fall and winter only. Contrary to conventional wisdom, Flycatchers were found more frequently and at higher densities in grazed patches than in ungrazed patches. We detected no significant effects of grazing on nest success or rate of brood parasitism. We suggest that this result is due to the type of progressive grazing management practiced on the U Bar Ranch.

# Balancing Weeds and Ranching

*by Duke Phillips*

Duke Phillips was raised on a large cattle ranch in Coahuila, Mexico, five hours from the nearest village. Throughout his twenties, Duke worked on ranches ranging from 20,000 acres grazing 1,500 cows to 2.75 million acres running 45,000 cows. Duke began his ranch management career in 1985 when he moved to the Cañon Blanco Ranch in White Rock, New Mexico. Today, Duke and his wife Janet live on the Chico Basin Ranch in Hanover, Colorado. He has strong working relationships with The Nature Conservancy, The Rocky Mountain Bird Observatory, and the Colorado Division of Wildlife. The ranch supports a diversified business that manages a seedstock Beefmaster cattle herd, a cattle grazing and management business, recreation, and education operations. The ranch has hosted over 3,500 visitors since 1999.

Economic hardship is the single most detrimental thing for the ecology of the land, no matter whether it comes in the form of drought, hungry grasshoppers, bad business decisions, or a depressed market. Weeds begin sprouting when the land is stressed. Weeds come in all different forms and sizes. And, weeds aren't necessarily plants. If we do not have a diverse and healthy business on a ranch, then the land usually takes it in the pants. When I begin seeing weeds, I wonder if perhaps they are a symptom of a ranching management program that is out of balance.

## Multi-Dimensional Resource

The Chico Basin Ranch is a new business outside Colorado Springs, Colorado, that operates on the premise that a ranch is a multi-dimensional resource, not just a home for a herd of cattle. I believe that this ranch is unique, as all ranches are in their own way, and that its intrinsic qualities can be leveraged to create a dynamic business that sustains the land and wildlife and maintains a lifestyle that the people living and working on the ranch can be proud of.

The Chico Basin Ranch is located between Colorado Springs and Pueblo, on the high desert prairie. It has three ecosystems:

20,000 acres of sand sage, roughly 3,000 acres of wetland/riparian, and 65,000 acres of short-grass prairie. It has 350 acres of irrigated farm land planted in alfalfa and permanent pasture for grazing, some haying, and upland bird habitat (hunting).

The ranch is owned by the Colorado State Land Board and is

learn more about ranching, and for agriculturalists who want to learn more about working with environmental groups and about better business practices.

I didn't realize how much live water, how much good exotic plant habitat, or good cow habitat or good deer habitat existed until I started

The Chico Basin Ranch. (All photos courtesy of Duke Phillips.)

leased by Duke and Janet Phillips, and our four children—Tess, Duke, Julie, and Grace—for a 25-year term, which began in 1999. The ranch operates strictly on cash flow and carries no debt. Ninety-five percent of the ranch's income comes from providing a turnkey grazing and management service to cattle owners. We also own a seed stock Beefmaster herd and have several non-traditional enterprises that are operated on the ranch. Additionally, we run about ten workshops throughout the year in collaboration with The Rocky Mountain Bird Observatory and The Nature Conservancy, and independently, for school kids of all ages, for the urban community wanting to

getting to know the ranch from horseback. Hidden draws with springs flowing out and traveling down through parched desert land, entirely different ecosystems intermingled in a patchwork across the ranch. The ranch hosts plenty of weeds along with several threatened and endangered plant and animal species and works with The Nature Conservancy, The Natural Heritage Program, and The Rocky Mountain Bird Observatory on their management.

We also work with Charley Orchard, Kirk Gadzia, and others on range monitoring and workshops aimed at improving our management skills and knowledge. Our objective is ultimately to have 30 transects across the ranch representative of various types of terrains and problems. Through the transects, we will track those species of plants, animals, and situations that have special needs or that represent opportunities. Additionally, we want to use the information to make better decisions about the natural environment and our business.

## Weed "Care"

As we look at the various things that we have to do, managing our exotic weed problem is one of our lowest priority tasks. I say this not because we don't have a lot of weeds—we do—but because if we spent too much time focused specifically on just one problem—in this case weeds—I believe we would go broke. Time is the most essential thing we have and is in the least supply. Consequently, we attempt to include weed "care" in our overall management scheme. Our philosophy in managing this business is challenging ourselves to identify and leverage the most promising inherent qualities of the ranch to create a healthy, diversified business that enhances our natural resources. We have found that the hard part has been keeping from getting distracted and being pulled in too many directions at one time. Consequently, today, we devote ourselves to five primary

profit centers that we think have the long-term potential of moving the cattle enterprise toward the background financially, and to serve more as a tool for managing the surface of the ground to achieve our conservation goals.

Checking out the ranch on horseback.

## Grazing Management

Managing our weeds is one small part of one aspect of one management area—grazing. A much larger challenge today is the pending prolonged drought and not getting caught with our pants down, even though it may turn out we can do nothing except pack up and leave. In anticipation of a prolonged drought, we hired Kirk Gadzia to come to the ranch to give a class on grazing planning. Our objective was to come away from it with a comprehensive grazing plan that allowed us to grow as much grass as possible without destocking.

Weed management came into the picture when we thought of inviting Lani Lamming to give a presentation on her weed-control

Headquarters Lake on the Chico Basin Ranch. The kids are fishing for bass and blue gill.

methods using goats, and because we have been interested in running goats together with our cattle. I thought also that, through her, we could get other people to the ranch to defray the costs of the school. Bob Painter from the Colorado Division of Wildlife (CDOW) also gave us a presentation to round things out; he is widely respected in eastern Colorado for his work with weed control on CDOW properties by using cattle grazing and minimal amounts of chemicals.

We came away from the course with a comprehensive grazing plan that included controlling our exotic plants. We also spent much time in small quarters, isolated from phones and interruptions from the outside talking about ranching,

grazing, weed control, grazing, management, ranching, diversification, grazing, and ranching. We ate a lot of good food, had a lot of laughs. I have thought many times since of how good it is to close oneself away with others of kindred mind to think in depth about things.

Another outcome of the course was our decision to graze 900 yearlings using portable fencing through our riparian and wetland areas in five- to 50-acre breaks (paddocks). Bob Painter's presentation convinced us that by simply grazing cattle in some kind of intensive fashion so that there was "tromping" (Bob's words) by the cattle's hooves, and rest, all or most of the weeds would disappear. So, we thought, if we *really* intensify the process, we would disturb the surface of the ground to increase the mineral and water cycles, succession, and energy flow—the exact things that we determined we needed to do in order to grow as much grass as possible. *And* we would manage our weeds, *and* we would graze each inch of ground for a very short time, between one and four days, to rest the remainder of the year.

### Goats, Too!

Toward the end of the workshop, as we sat digesting our

major decision to graze a large herd of cattle in such an intensive manner, the prospect of grazing Lani's goat herd with our cows as an experiment started burning hotter. I have always fantasized about one day tearing out all the fences on this ranch and grazing a multi-species herd consisting of cattle, goats, and sheep, all with the same labor force it would take to graze only the cattle, in a migratory fashion around the range: a covered wagon with a cowboy crew supported by dogs, horses, ultralights, and motorcycles caring for the land and livestock; another crew on the other side of the pasture bringing vacationers out from around the world to help herd the 15,000-head herd; busloads of school kids with another crew in another part of the pasture coming out to learn about ranching and the ecosystem. And Lani had always wondered about the dynamics of grazing goats with cattle.

Kirk thought the idea was such an important one in terms of gaining knowledge about grazing that he contributed $1,000 toward the experiment. It just turned out that we got along great with Lani (who wouldn't?), and Lani, with some time in between jobs, decided to graze her 700 head of goats here for several weeks as an experiment, which, today, is all history.

It was great fun. We grazed the livestock in three ways: cattle in front of the goats, goats in front of the cattle, and together, loose herding them. We made Land EKG (Charley Orchard) transects across each area,

as well as across an area that neither goats nor cattle had grazed, as a control area. The goats worked well with the cattle, as they chose the woody plants and liked diving off the banks of the arroyos (breaking down the banks), and the cattle affected a relatively much larger ground surface area. We will know much more next year when we re-analyze the transects.

## Thinking Evolved

The cattle today continue grazing in the small areas, old hands to the routine of moving regularly, eating all varieties of plants, except tamarisk and Russian olive (we miss the goats). Our thinking has evolved considerably since that long day at the end of our workshop. We are contemplating grazing our entire herd of cows with portable fencing through the ranch to accomplish several things: **first**, but not necessarily in order of importance, it would control the weeds—we see this as a side benefit; **second**, we would enhance the ecosystem as much as it can possibly be enhanced; **third**, it would position us to manage the ecosystem processes to the fullest extent that we know in order to get through the drought; **fourth**, we would learn the maximum amount about grazing this land; **fifth**, we would be able to better control the nutritional plane of the livestock; **sixth**, we would learn exactly the production capability of the land so that when we come through on the other side of the drought, we can more correctly stock our country. All in all, it means taking things to the edge in order to learn as much as possible about grazing management.

Wannes de Lange, from Holland, is holding a bird that was caught in a net that The Rocky Mountain Bird Observatory put up in their April and May bird banding station on the ranch to get school kids out to the ranch to see birds. Wannes was working at Chico Basin and then joined Lani Lamming in New Mexico for a couple of months to help her herd her goats.

It means becoming as intimate as possible with the land, which is the basis for all activities that support our lives on this ranch.

### Importance of Management

Lately, as I have attended grazing and ranching conferences outside the agriculture industry, the buzz has been that *ranching can actually be good for the ecosystem.* These conferences remind us all of the importance of **management**, as in all businesses, but which for some reason is underestimated in ranching. In the normal course of my business though, I do not consciously think about the positive things that I strive to do for the land in my care, because I crossed that road such a long time ago, and it is the core part of what we do.

I spend more time thinking of those things that help stabilize my business during the erratic climatic swings, or the dramatic rise and fall of markets, or from misaligned perceptions. When speaking to environmental advocacy and cattle grower groups, I talk about building a diversified business, about working together with ecologists instead of dropping into our comfortable adversarial pose. I usually forget to say anything about our land steward-ship work, because protecting and enhancing the land is simply part of our routine, part of the process of our ranching practices that go back further than I care to remember these days.

In all of our personal lives and in all life on this ranch, Mother Nature is where everything starts and where everything ends. This one fact colors everything that we do in our business. "Weeds" are simply a manifestation of what we don't want to happen. It is dangerous getting carried away chasing them off. If we keep our focus on what we desire, on our dreams, on our fantasies, and if we attempt to work together toward our mutual goals instead of focusing on our differences, then the weeds will drop out of the landscape of our land and business, and out of our lives. And that will leave more time to enjoy the things we like, which, for me, is the tranquility that comes with living and working with land and animals on a ranch.

# Herding: How it Works in the West Elks

*by Dave Bradford and Steve Allen*

Dave Bradford [right] is the range and wildlife staff officer on the Paonia Ranger District, Gunnison National Forest. He has worked in Paonia since 1993 and for the Forest Service since 1981. He has been president of the Colorado Section, Society for Range Management.

Steve Allen [see photo on page 40] is one of seven permittees on the West Elk allotment. Steve and his wife Rachel have ranched on Fruitland Mesa and the West Elk allotment since 1987. Steve is on the Board of Directors of the Colorado Branch for Holistic Management.

Like most things in life, ranching is changing. Whether we accept it or not, like it or not, changes are occurring. With some changes, the benefits are easily seen and consequently readily accepted. With other changes, the benefits are not so obvious and, as a result, may not be accepted at all, unless the change is forced upon us. On the Western Slope of Colorado over the past five to ten years, there have been a number of changes in how ranchers manage their operations. Some of these changes have occurred because they were willingly adopted, some because there was no choice.

One change that is increasingly being adopted by Western Slope ranchers is the practice of herding cattle. Herding can be described as a management tech-nique where livestock are kept as a more-or-less single unit as they graze. Generally this technique is part of an overall management approach that is sometimes called planned grazing or holistic management. The planning is critical, as all management techniques that are used in grazing need to be considered as part of an overall goal. The West Elk Livestock Association has used herding as part of their grazing plans since the early 1990s, and the approach has been a resounding success. The success on the West Elk has helped planned grazing and herding to spread throughout Western Colorado.

## Setting

The West Elk allotment is located in the North Fork of the Gunnison River Valley in western

Colorado, southeast of the town of Paonia. The North Fork Valley is both rural and lightly populated. The economy is based on coal

Steve Allen [left] resting in a recently grazed pasture in the West Elks Wilderness. (Photo courtesy of Courtney White.)

mining, fruit orchards, and livestock ranching.

The allotment lies in the northwest portion of the West Elk Mountains. The northern West Elk Mountains were created 10 to 50 million years ago as orogenic processes forced intrusions of igneous materials up through the surrounding sedimentary deposits of shales and sandstones. This created a complex landscape of cone-shaped, igneous mountains interspersed with basins, ridges, and slopes of shales and sandstones. Elevations vary from 6,000 to 12,000 feet. The precipitation also varies—with the lowest elevations receiving an average of seven inches per year and the highest elevations receiving over 40

inches. The vegetation on the allotment varies with elevation and topography. The lowest elevation areas are desert adobe hills and washes on the western side of the allotment. Lying to the east of the shale hills are mesas covered with juniper-piñon woodlands. Further east and increasing in elevation are the lower mountain slopes blanketed with oakbrush and serviceberry. Above these areas are aspen-cloaked slopes and ridges and further above them are subalpine parks. The allotment covers 90,000 acres. There are approximately 5,000 acres of Bureau of Land Management (BLM) land and 85,000 acres of Gunnison National Forest (FS)—with 60,000 acres of this in the West Elk Wilderness.

## History

Six ranching families hold seven grazing permits on the West Elk allotment. They run their livestock as a cattle pool. While livestock grazing has been going on in the West Elk Mountains for over 100 years, the West Elk allotment had its beginnings in 1981 when four separate allotments were combined on a trial basis. The combination was also the beginning of grazing this area with a single herd.

The trial combination was formalized in 1986. From 1986 to

1993, the allotment followed a deferred-rotation grazing strategy, based on leaving a percentage of forage in a grazing unit by grazing each unit for a specific period of time. This approach has some benefits but can be overly rigid and generally does not consider plant growth and regrowth. It also does not consider other factors that may be important, such as poisonous plants, wildlife calving/nesting areas, recreation use, permittee activities, rare/threatened/endangered plants or animals, etc. In 1994, the permittees, the BLM, and the Forest Service initiated an allotment plan based on holistic management. Like most allotment management plans (AMP) on public lands, the West Elk AMP has objectives, management actions, range improvements, and monitoring. But it is also based on a Three-part Goal which defines the end product that management is directed toward. The elements of such a Goal are: 1) Quality of Life; 2) Description of Forms of Production; and 3) Landscape Description. The goal of the West Elk allotment follows:

### West Elk Allotment Management Goal

"1. *Quality of Life.* From now and into the future, our goal is to maintain a safe, secure, rural community with economic, social, and biological diversity. We will promote a community that respects individual freedom and values education, and that encourages cooperation. We agree to act as good

stewards in maintaining a healthy ecosystem in the West Elk allotment

Portable water troughs help keep cattle out of riparian areas. (Photo courtesy of Dave Bradford.)

and enjoy doing it.

"2. *Forms of Production.* Our stewardship of the West Elk allotment and Wilderness Area will foster abundant and diverse flora and fauna, clean air and water, and stable soils. From this, the local population can derive a stable livelihood, and local residents and visitors can enjoy the aesthetic and natural values of the area.

"3. *Landscape.* Our landscape covers adobe ground, brushy mid-ground, and mountain environments, including many different

---

habitat types that we are committed to maintaining. Our goal is to have a good water cycle by having close plant spacing, a covered soil surface, and arable soils; have a fast mineral

Temporary electric fence used to hold cattle out of giant Larkspur. (Photo courtesy of Dave Bradford.)

cycle using soil nutrients effectively; have an energy flow that maximizes the amount of sunlight converted to plant growth and values the seclusion and natural aesthetics of the area."

All management actions are evaluated against this goal to ensure that good decisions are made in the planning stage and that funds and efforts are expended only on actions that will help accomplish the goal. The grazing plans for each year are developed at an open meeting. Anyone with an interest in grazing on the West Elk allotment is invited to attend. The specific details for grazing on the allotment that year are developed at the meeting, including livestock numbers, the grazing season, pasture sequence, grazing

levels, mitigation measures, range improvements, and monitoring. Livestock numbers are based on the original Term Permits of 1,056 cow/calf pairs, but may vary—in 1998 the pool ran an additional 200 yearlings. The grazing season also varies but can occur within a May 10 to November 30 period. The grazing schedule generally includes 30 grazing units. Livestock moves between pastures are scheduled from three to 20 days—based on the biological plan. Actual moves are based on on-the-ground conditions. It's important to realize that livestock are moved before plants can begin to regrow. This is an important factor in ensuring that the range is not overgrazed. The planned grazing and herding provides the control needed to meet the management goal.

## Herding

One of the key tools in moving toward the allotment goal has been the management of the livestock as a single herd. This single herd approach allows the permittees to concentrate their energies on all of the cattle at one time. Managing livestock as a single herd allows the permittees to more easily monitor what their livestock are doing. While there is a grazing schedule, the actual livestock moves are based on what is happening out on the ground.

How are livestock managed as a single herd on the West Elk

allotment? The process resembles a large flowing body in nearly continuous movement across the landscape. The herd can be described as a body with a head and a tail. Those cattle that are always pushing into new areas are the head. These are followed by the large mass of cattle that are the body. And the stragglers, that want to stay in the grazed pastures, are the tail. Cattle moves are almost never accomplished by moving 1,056 cow/calf pairs as a single unit. The pool riders accomplish moves by guiding the head of the herd, or the leaders, into the areas that are planned for grazing. These leaders are usually followed by the body of the herd, moving on their own. The stragglers are then pushed along with the rest of the herd.

While most pasture moves involve moving into adjacent grazing units, several of the moves involve trailing the herd long distances—from five to ten miles—and through formidable physical barriers. Originally the permittees thought that it would take one rider for each 50 pairs. Consequently they gathered up 20 or so riders to help in the moves.

Over time they found that this many riders causes a great amount of confusion. Today the group uses no more than six riders for these moves.

The density of the herd varies between pastures and within each pasture. There could be 10 pairs

Cows being herded in the West Elks Wilderness. Herding has allowed miles of barbed wire fence to be removed. (Photo courtesy of the West Elk Grazing Association.)

scattered over one-half acre or 50 pairs grazing on one acre. Twenty minutes later this large group might disperse. There is continuous movement throughout the unit. Remember that, since the livestock are being managed as a single herd, they're limited to 1/30th of the allotment at any one time.

Some years, the pool has used a hired rider, with supplemental riding by the permittees. Other years, the pool has hired one of the permittees as the pool rider. And one year the pool split the riding duties among the various permittees.

We continue to experiment with various options. However, there are a number of techniques that we believe help to accomplish the job:

1) Approach livestock calmly and don't push.

**Before:** The West Elks in the 1920s. An example of historic overgrazing (note the trees). (Photo courtesy of Dave Bradford.)

2) Point the livestock in the right direction and let them walk there.

3) Use good stock dogs. We use Border Collies.

4) Use salt effectively:

a) Focus on using salt as an attractant. On most western range-lands, salt is not required as a nutritional supplement, but it is highly desired by livestock.

b) Reduce the amount of salt used—we went from 5 tons per year to 1 ton.

c) Time spent putting out salt can be more effectively used herding.

d) Less salt seems to help reduce the incidence of "brisket" and other high elevation problems.

5) Some fencing may be necessary, but keep in mind that no fence will hold a hungry cow. For a variety of reasons, we use some hard, four-wire fences, some fences with permanent posts and temporary electric ribbon, and some temporary electric fence with portable posts. The temporary electric fence offers flexibility and can reinforce our riding efforts where control is difficult.

Our on-the-ground management changes as we continue to learn. It will probably never be completely set, as conditions change, people change, and the land changes.

## Why Are You Doing This? What's In It For Me?

For most of us, this is the basic question—the bottom line. Why should I consider making this change? We believe there are a number of reasons:

1) This approach provides flexibility on the ground. Planned grazing provides many more opportunities for flexibility in management. One example involves range readiness. By having many grazing units, there are many adjustments that can be made for changing weather conditions. A number of years, we have had cool wet springs. This has delayed plant growth in the high country. We were able to stay a day longer in seven of the early

pastures. This gave us a week extra for the high country to develop, before we moved there. And since the year was wet, there was good plant regrowth as we moved on and out of these early pastures.

2) Cattle performance has improved. Some of this is due to genetic improvements, but overall calf weights have increased 50 to 100 pounds. Our weaning weights vary from 550 to 650 pounds, depending on the genetics of the individual's herd. The number of open cows has also decreased, as we do a better job of keeping the bulls with the cows. Our open cows vary from 5 to 8%. Our vet bills have also declined. We attribute all of this to keeping the cattle on fresh feed and using short low-stress moves. We have heard of concerns that moving cattle frequently will reduce their weight gains. We haven't seen that. We have seen that, when we have inadvertently left some cattle behind, they weighed 50 pounds less than the rest of the herd.

3) Relationships with other ranchers have improved. Working towards a common goal helps us to stay focused on the important things.

4) Range conditions have improved. Herding has improved range distribution/utilization. There are fewer "overgrazed/undergrazed" areas. When we herd our cattle, we are doing a better job of managing grazing. By controlling when we

**After:** The West Elks in the 1990s. An example of the benefit of planned grazing. (Photo courtesy of Dave Bradford.)

graze and how much we graze, plants are able to get the regrowth they need to maintain themselves.

5) This is a quality of life issue. A major reason we do this is that we perceive ourselves to be horseback ranchers.

## Costs

There are major costs associated with running our cattle on the West Elk allotment. Our pool fees for 1998 were $2.50 per cow per month, $3.85 with grazing fee. This figures to $11.00 per cow for the season, $16.94 with grazing fees. Our pool fees are "out-of-pocket" expenses, such as salt, grain for the

The West Elk Livestock Association has received a number of awards in recognition of their management. They received the Colorado Section, Society for Range Management's 1996 Excellence in Rangeland Conservation Award. In 1997, they were awarded a Land Stewardship Award from the Western Slope Environmental Resource Coalition, an environmental group in the North Fork Valley. In 1997, the Forest Service awarded the group the Chief's Award for Excellence in Range Management.

horses, food for the riders. This is the lowest cost we've had. We did all our own riding in 1998. If we had hired a pool rider, you could include another $2.00 per head per month, or $5,000 for the season.

If these reasons appeal to you and you think you might be interested in giving this approach a try, we have some suggestions.

### Tips For Making It Work

1) Base grazing plans on a biological approach—there are known seasons, opportunities, limitations, needs, and difficulties that can be planned for in advance.

2) Collaborate rather than fight—it is more productive.

3) Start the process quickly—don't get bogged down on details.

4) Assume you can be wrong and monitor to see if you are.

5) Plan on having at least one wreck—things can and do go wrong. Nothing always works perfectly, so it ain't a mistake if you don't repeat it.

6) Schedule meetings every year. Deal with issues/problems before they become major road-blocks.

7) Don't fixate on the little problems. It is critical to have a goal so you know where you are going and to help you determine what is a little or big problem.

8) Remember that all plans are temporary and can be changed.

Will planned grazing using herding work for you? We can't say with absolute certainty that it will. However, it has worked successfully for us, and we believe it will work for others. This approach is being used successfully on over a dozen grazing allotments in Western Colorado. We believe it is an excellent approach to grazing livestock, that has worked wherever we have seen it tried. Do we recommend it? Absolutely.

# Conservation in the Radical Center

# Looking for the "Radical Center"

*by William de Buys*

W illiam deBuys is an author, educator, and historian. He holds a Ph.D. in American Studies from the University of Texas at Austin. He is the author of *Enchantment and Exploitation: The Life and Hard Times of a New Mexico Mountain Range, River of Traps: A Village Life* (with Alex Harris), *Salt Dreams: Land and Water in Low-Down California* (with Joan Myers). He is currently director of The Conservation Fund's Valle Grande Grass Bank on Rowe Mesa, near Santa Fe, and chair of the Valles Caldera National Preserve Board of Trustees.

I first heard the term "Radical Center" from Bill McDonald, one of the founders of the Malpai Borderlands Group. When I asked him whether he'd made it up or heard it somewhere else, he said he couldn't remember and that people should use the term freely.

Bill used "Radical Center" to describe the political and social domain in which the Malpai Group carries out its work. The core of the organization consists of a grassroots alliance of ranchers who realized they needed help dealing with the labyrinth of agencies and regulations governing use of the country they depended on. In particular, they knew that they needed to pursue a different and more naturalistic kind of fire regime throughout the lands where their cattle grazed, that they had to fight the encroachment of subdivisions that would fragment their landscape, that it was essential to improve the quality of science on which management decisions for public lands were based, and in general that they needed to strengthen the economic foundations of ranching in their area. Their ultimate goals were to preserve their way of life and to restore the large landscapes in which they lived. And they knew very well that those two goals were really just one. Their breakthrough, conceptually and politically, was to reach out and form alliances with The Nature Conservancy, an environmental group that most ranchers viewed as an enemy, and with federal agencies, like the Forest Service and the Bureau of Land Management (BLM), that their neighbors typically viewed with equal scorn.

### Breakthrough

The Nature Conservancy also experienced a breakthrough in its thinking. As its people grappled with the complexities of owning and

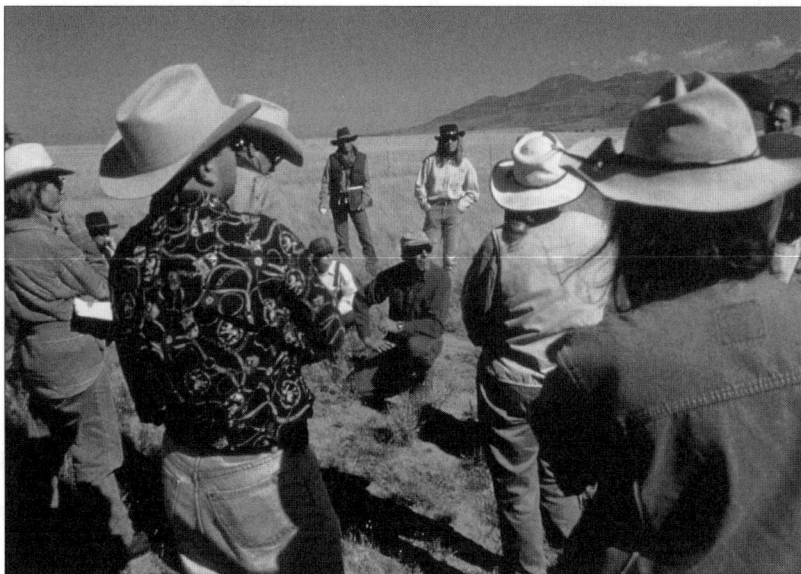

In the Radical Center, we can "take on partners we never thought we'd be working with." At the Gray Ranch. (Photo courtesy of Courtney White.)

later reselling the sprawling Gray Ranch, they realized that, if they wanted to preserve the diversity of large landscapes, they had to work constructively and meaningfully with the people who inhabited and used those landscapes.

The Radical Center is where the Conservancy and the ranchers of the Malpai region came together. It's a place where people agree that business as usual isn't working. For ranchers, it involves realizing that they can't survive alone; they must find partners for the sake of having rich new ideas and programs and funds and cutting through red tape. They needed to work with other

people for the sake of getting their message out to a broader audience. Of utmost importance, however, was the fact that the message had changed. The Malpai ranchers understood and accepted that their generation must attain a higher level of environmental performance than previous generations thought necessary. Society insisted on it. The old norms, by themselves, didn't cut it anymore.

### Departure

For environmentalists, the Radical Center required a similar departure from old habits. If enviros want to protect the land and restore and maintain its diversity, they've got to find a way to work constructively with people. The old business of saying, "Our way is the only way, so do it our way or be sued," won't lead to a widely shared societal ethic of environmental stewardship. You don't get people to adopt an ethic by beating them over the head with your version while pretending they have none of their own. In the Radical Center, environmentalists learn as much, if not more, than they teach.

There is a third generalized group in the Radical Center. They are the agency folks from the Forest Service, Cooperative Extension, BLM, Natural Resources Conservation Service (NRCS)—the list is long—who are frustrated with sacrificing their professional lives to lawsuits and who are ready to take action and risks in order to get needed work done on the ground. They don't get bogged down defending procedure; instead they find ways to make real things happen.

There is plenty of room for others in the Radical Center, including scientists who dedicate themselves to place-based learning that illuminates core problems of day-to-day, pragmatic land management, and consumers, who consciously use their spending power to support producers who ranch and farm to the highest standards.

## Work in the Radical Center

Work that takes place in the Radical Center might be said to have four principal characteristics:

1. It involves a departure from business as usual.

2. It is not bigoted. By that, I mean that, to do this kind of work, you don't question where somebody is from or what kind of hat he or she wears, you focus on where that person is willing to go and whether he or she is willing to work constructively on matters of mutual interest.

3. Work in the Radical Center also involves a commitment to using a diversity of tools. There is not one way of doing things. There can be many ways of doing things. We need to have large toolboxes and to lend and borrow tools freely.

4. Work in the Radical Center is experimental—it keeps developing new alternatives every

step along the way. Nothing is ever so good that it can't stand a little revision, and nothing is ever so impossible and broken down that a try at fixing it is out of the question.

These days, we've basically got two major modes of working on environmental issues. We read about one of them in the newspaper virtually every day—it is argumentative and rights-based. "I have the right to this. You don't have the right to that. I'm going to enforce my right by redefining your responsibility to respect my right."

The other mode is the mode of the Radical Center. It's the mode

> "We all need to know what our rights are. But at the same time, we also need to keep in mind what our interests are. And when we are smart enough to separate our interests from our political positions, then we can do some really good work."

of The Quivira Coalition. It is collaborative and interest-based. We all need to know what our rights are. But at the same time, we also need to keep in mind what our interests are. And when we are smart enough to separate our interests from our political positions, then we can do some really good work. Then we can have the flexibility to experiment, to innovate, to make mid-course corrections, to take on partners we never thought we'd be working with, and so on.

## Change

One of the reasons the adaptive, experimental style of the Radical Center is so important is that any difficult task, certainly the task of trying to save and restore land, is a little bit like trying to land an airplane on a revolving runway. Things are always changing, including the land itself. We know, for instance, that in northern New Mexico, we've lost over 50% of the grassy element of the ecological mosaic in the last 50 or 60 years. Similar changes are true of many other regions of the West. We have to work with those changes if we are going to maintain traditional public land grazing. We've got to open the uplands back up. We've got to get fire back into the system. If we do that, the results will be good for all species that depend on grasslands, from jackrabbits and juncos to curlews and cowboys.

No less than the land, society is also changing. Society's standards for environmental performance are different today from what they were in the 1960s. The bar has been raised. And it is going to continue to be raised. The person, or the group, or the business that's going to be effective five years from now, ten years from now, will be keeping an eye on the ways society changes and will be ready for them.

The best way to contend with these changes is to live alertly and attentively. This requires learning continually. It is the only way that we're going to preserve our working relationships to the land, together with the heritage that comes with those relationships. It is the only way, in fact, that we're going to be able to keep large landscapes intact for their ecological values and to prevent either their abandonment (which is hardly the same as restoration) or their colonization and fragmentation by exurban expansion.

# A New Environmentalism

*by Courtney White*

Courtney White is executive director of The Quivira Coalition. He has been a professional archaeologist for many years, employed with the National Park Service and other institutions. In 1994, he became active within the environmental movement, eventually becoming a leader in the local group of the Sierra Club. In 1997, he co-founded The Quivira Coalition with a rancher and another conservationist, in an effort to find common ground in the increasingly fractious debate about the future of grazing in the American West.

For as long as I can remember, environmentalists have been trying to tell ranchers what to do.

When I was a young backpacker in the late 1970s, dodging cow pies in the wilderness, the message was blunt: "Stop overgrazing our public range!" Today, the scolding by environmentalists has become more sophisticated, though also more strident, with some of it focused on abolishing public lands ranching altogether.

Even those who believe that ranching can be done in an ecologically sustainable manner are calling for significant changes in the way most ranches are managed, albeit through a collaborative, problem-solving process.

Either way, environmentalists have demanded that ranchers shoulder a great deal of the economic and emotional cost of change without providing much in the way of financial, physical, or moral support at the same time.

Nor have environmentalists challenged their own core paradigms in any way approximating the scale asked of ranchers. Activists are quick to lecture ranchers about the march of progress, but slow to admit that new thinking, changing technologies, and shifting societal values are challenging public lands environmentalism at a fundamental level as well. Suing on process and procedure, for example, today produces far more conflict than it does clean water or healthy habitat.

The time has come for environmentalists to share the burden of change, and not just financially, but intellectually. This means trying a fundamentally new approach to public lands activism, one that I believe involves a focus on land health, restoration, collaboration, creating and measuring results,

Rangeland health map of the Altar Valley. (All photos courtesy of Courtney White, unless otherwise noted.)

## Rangeland Health

The potential of a fresh approach became clear to me last spring when my friend Nathan Sayre gave me a new map of the 500,000-acre Altar Valley, located south of Tucson, Arizona. Commissioned by an alliance of ranchers concerned about the spread of Tucson's sprawl in their direction, funded by a state grant, and subcontracted to a private consulting firm, the map was important for what it measured: indicators of rangeland health.

Drawn up in seven colors, the map expressed the intersection of three variables: soil stability, biotic integrity, and watershed function (soil, grass, and water). It displayed three conditions for each variable: stable, at risk, and unstable. A color was chosen to represent a particular intersection. For example, deep red designated an "unstable," or unhealthy, condition for soil, grass, and water, while deep green represented "stable" for all three. Other colors represented conditions between these extremes.

and sharing resources.

Much of the private property on the west side of the valley (there is very little federal land in the watershed), which is actively managed, was dark green, while land on the east side, which is generally owned *in absentia,* was a patchwork of yellows and oranges, especially along the arroyos.

Smack in the middle of the map was a large private ranch called the Palo Alto. When I visited it last fall, I was shocked by its condition. It had been overgrazed to the point of being nearly "cowburnt," to use Edward Abbey's famous phrase. As one might expect, the color of the Palo Alto on the map was blood red, and there was plenty of it. By the criteria of rangeland health—soil, grass, and water—the Palo Alto was in trouble. And it was easy it see why.

A short distance down on the map, abutting the southern boundary of the Palo Alto, was another big splotch of dark red. This was no ranch, however. This was the Buenos Aires National Wildlife Refuge—a large chunk of protected land that had been cattle-free for nearly sixteen years. I visited the refuge as well, learning that the refuge managers have an active prescribed fire program, and have tried various mitigation strategies to retard persistent soil erosion. From the perspective of rangeland health, however, these strategies were not proving effective.

I arranged to meet Walt Meyer, the man who did the field work for the map. A rancher with a Ph.D. in range ecology, Walt said he read 500 transects across the Altar Valley, using a range-land health system that graded sites on the degree to which they deviated from an ideal ecological site type. He said the problem on the Buenos Aires wasn't the proliferation of exotic Lehmann's lovegrass, because it was only one variable out of many. Instead, it was a combination of things, principally soil erosion, that pushed the upper portion of the refuge into the red. And he stood by his analysis.

As I learned more, I began to appreciate how the Altar Valley map, and the rangeland health paradigm it employed, exposed us to the question of ecological functionality in a way that challenged our cherished beliefs about the intrinsic sanctity of "protected areas."

I learned this the hard way one day as I began to describe the map, and its implications, to a diverse group of people sitting under a tree at a workshop on the Gila National Forest. As I began to talk about the wildlife refuge, a young environmentalist from Tucson took offense at the suggestion that the refuge might be un-healthy in any way and cut me off. Rudely, too. Clearly, I had strayed

too close to a core belief—that "protected areas," such as parks, wilderness areas, and wildlife refuges, could possibly be in poor ecological condition.

In her reaction, I saw the confirmation of the need for a new environmentalism.

[Top] The Palo Alto Ranch in the Altar Valley. [Bottom] The Buenos Aires National Wildlife Refuge.

## Soil First!

The concept behind range-land health is a powerful and promising paradigm for a new activism. Its underlying idea is a simple one: that before land can support a value, such as livestock grazing, hunting, recreation, or wildlife protection, it must be at least in proper functioning condition. In other words, before we, as a society, can talk about designating critical habitat for endangered species, or increasing forage for cows, or expanding recreational use, we need to know the answer to a simple question: Is the land healthy at the level of soil, grass, and water? If the answer is "no," then all our values may be at risk.

But what is "health" exactly? In 1994, the National Academy of Sciences published a book entitled *Rangeland Health: New Methods to Classify, Inventory, and Monitor Rangelands*.[1] In it, the authors define range health as "the degree to which the integrity of the soil and the ecological processes of rangelands ecosystems are sustained." They go on to say, "The capacity of range-lands to produce commodities and to satisfy values on a sustained basis depends on internal, self-sustaining ecological processes such as soil development, nutrient cycling, energy flow, and the structure and dynamics of plant and animal communities."

Or, as Kirk Gadzia, one of the book's co-authors, likes to put it, "It all comes down to soil. If it's stable, there's hope for the future. But if it's moving, then all bets are off for the ecosystem." It is a sentiment echoed by Roger Bowe, an award-winning rancher from eastern New Mexico, who says, "Bare soil is the rancher's number one enemy."

I think it should also become the number one enemy of environmentalists as well.

The publication of *Rangeland Health* was the touchstone for a new approach within the scientific communities. It paved the way for the debut last year of a federal inter-agency publication entitled *Interpreting Indicators of Rangeland Health*[2] which provides a 17-point checklist for the **qualitative** assessment of upland health. A method for **quantifying** rangeland health has just been produced by scientists at the USDA's Jornada Experimental Station, located near Las Cruces, New Mexico.[3]

Taken together, these methods are new and valuable tools for measuring the ecological condition of our uplands.

A similar approach was developed by the interagency Na-

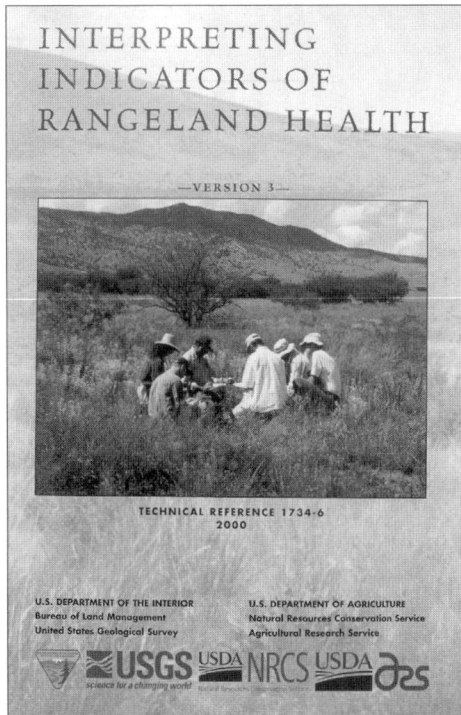

INTERPRETING INDICATORS OF RANGELAND HEALTH

—VERSION 3—

TECHNICAL REFERENCE 1734-6
2000

U.S. DEPARTMENT OF THE INTERIOR
Bureau of Land Management
United States Geological Survey

U.S. DEPARTMENT OF AGRICULTURE
Natural Resources Conservation Service
Agricultural Research Service

USGS    USDA NRCS    USDA ars

tional Riparian Team. Their own seventeen-point checklist assesses the physical functioning of riparian and wetland areas through "consideration of hydrology, vegetation, and soil/ landform attributes." The goal of this assessment, which the National Riparian Team calls Proper Functioning Condition (PFC),[4] is "to provide information on whether a riparian-wetland area is physically functioning in a manner which will allow the maintenance or recovery of **desired values**, e.g., fish habitat, neotropical birds, or forage, over time." [*Emphasis added.*]

Many years ago, Aldo Leopold lamented that, "The art of land doctoring is being practiced with vigor, but the science of land health is yet to be born."[5] Now that a consensus has emerged among scientists and federal land managers on functionality and how to measure land health, I think we can say it **has** been born, with important implications for environmentalists, ranchers, and federal and state land managers.

A new environmentalism, in other words, is all about measuring and monitoring the land.

## Knowledge

Two summers ago I found myself sitting around a campfire at the CS Ranch thinking about ethics. I believed at the time, as I suspect many environmentalists do, that the chore of ending overgrazing in the West was a matter of getting ranchers to adopt an ecological ethic along the lines of those proposed by Mr.

Leopold in his famous essay. The question was, how?

I decided to ask Julia Davis, our host, for advice. A dozen years ago, Julia and her sister Kim talked their family into switching to holistic ranch management on the 100,000-acre CS, a decision that has caused the ranch to flourish economically and ecologically. Earlier in the day, I had been impressed by the sight of

"The only progress that counts is that on the actual landscape of the back forty."—Aldo Leopold

new beaver dams on a portion of the Cimarron River running through the CS, and also by Julia's support for their presence.

The Davis family, it seemed to me, had embraced Leopold's land ethic big time. So, I asked Julia: "How do we get other ranchers to change their ethics, too?"

Her answer completely rearranged my thinking.

"We didn't change our ethics," she replied. "We're the same ranchers we were 15 years ago. What changed was our knowledge. We went back to school, and we came back to the ranch with new ideas."

This is an incredibly important point. Knowledge, not ethics, is the key to good land stewardship. Over the past four years, I have had the good fortune to see many well-managed ranches (and some poor ones) in a wide variety of terrains. I've met a wide diversity of ranchers as well; and what I have learned is this: ranchers **do** have an environmental ethic, as they have claimed

**Before**: Macho Creek near Deming, New Mexico, in May 1998, before dormant season grazing was instituted.

for so long. Often, in fact, their ethic is a powerful one. What may be missing, however, is knowledge.

The same thing is true of many environmentalists (and many federal and state land managers). It has been, after all, a long time since many of us were in school. And in my experience, when old knowledge wears out it morphs into something that sounds suspiciously like dogma.

If we could go back to school, as the Davis family had the courage to do, what would we study? Aldo Leopold had a suggestion: the fundamentals of land health, which he described as "the capacity of the land for self-renewal." He also described the business of conservation as "our effort to understand and preserve this capacity."

Wendell Berry also has an

idea: Study the link between economics, culture, and land. He has written, "The two great ruiners of privately owned land are ignorance and economic constraint. And these tend to be related. People have ruined land mainly by overusing it—by forcing it to produce beyond its power to recover…and behind this overuse, almost always, has been economic need."[6] The same thing could be said of public land.

Environmentalists could also learn from the scientific community, as I did, that grazing is a natural process. The grazing of grass by ungulates has been going on in North America for at least 66 million years. The relationship between grass and grazers, while perhaps not entirely mutualistic, can be ecologically sustainable.[7]

Livestock grazing can also be a natural, and regenerative, form of ecological disturbance. That makes grazing significantly different from mining, clearcutting, or dam-building—an important point that environmentalists need to understand and acknowledge as a first step to more effective activism.

That requires, however, letting go of some bovine bigotry. A new environmentalism responds to the oft-cited charge that cattle are not "natural" by asking: Shouldn't our primary focus be on ecological processes—water cycling, nutrient cycling, energy flow—and how all our actions affect these processes on the ground? Using the criteria of rangeland health, I wonder which would be measured as more "unnatural"—a herd of cows or Phoenix, Arizona?

## Sanctuaries

What if the "value" we seek, however, is protection from human use altogether? Recently, an alternative school of "new environmentalism" has emerged, one that advocates for "unmanaged landscapes" and a return of "nature's autonomy." As Bill Willers has written, "When a living system becomes fragmented or manipulated, its internal pattern of relationships is destroyed. When managed for some human-centered purpose, its autonomy is lost. Restoring wilderness conditions on landscapes of all sizes can allow for self-regulation in a state of ancestral wholeness."

He further states that "there is no middle ground. If that which has functioned beautifully through the eons free of human meddling is to survive, 'management' must become an erasing, a reversing, a minimizing of human impact—a science of letting things be."[8]

The goal of this approach is to expand substantially the size of protected areas—parks, refuges, and wildernesses—and to significantly decrease human activity at the same time. The aim is to "rewild" native landscapes, principally through the

After: Macho Creek in September 2000. Bird surveys have shown significant increases in bird populations.

reintroduction of keystone predator species.

As attractive as this approach sounds, it has a serious flaw. What about functionality? What about soil, grass, and water? What chance do these predators have if their habitat is sick? Looking at this important issue through the prism of a "rangeland health" paradigm, a fundamental philosophical question arises: Can land be "wild" if it is not healthy?

This is a critical question because much of the history of the conservation movement has been focused on an effort to protect "wild" nature from destructive human use. Early on, the drive to preserve wilderness had its roots in culture—a romanticization of the nation's frontier period, an appeal to virility, and a fascination with the primitive. But with the development of the science of ecology, wilderness took on the role of ecological laboratory and wildlife sanctuary. For Aldo Leopold, a co-founder of The Wil-

**Before:** Upper Cottonwood, May 1928, West Elks national forest land near Paonia, Colorado. (Photo courtesy of the U.S.F.S.)

derness Society, one of the principal assets of wild land was to serve as "a base-datum of normality, a picture of how healthy land maintains itself as an organism."

And to preserve this "normality" land needed protection. Wallace Stegner, speaking for many of his generation, wrote, "Wildlife sanctuaries, national seashores and lakeshores, wild and scenic rivers, wilderness areas created under the 1964 Wilderness Act, all represent a strengthening of the decision to hold onto land and manage large sections of the public domain rather than dispose of them or let them *deteriorate.*"[9] [*Emphasis added.*]

The point is, this was decades ago. As the Altar Valley map implies, our "sanctuaries" may, in fact, no longer be the "reservoir of normal ecological processes," as Leopold imagined. From a rangeland health perspective, they may be deteriorating right before our eyes at the level of soil, grass, and water. Historic abuse, current mismanagement, or some other factor may be undermin-

ing the integrity of these places. For example, how do we shield the "natural autonomy" of wilderness areas and national parks from the effects of global warming, acid rain, and $CO_2$ buildup?

A recent paper in the journal *Wild Earth*, co-authored by Dr. Craig Allen, an ecologist with the USGS stationed at Bandelier, brings this issue into sharp relief—with significant implications for the future of the environmental movement on public lands.[10]

The paper examined the 30,000-acre federally designated wilderness area within Bandelier National Monument, located near Los Alamos, New Mexico, and declared it to be suffering from "unnatural change." And the problem, he finds, is not confined to Bandelier. "Most wilderness areas in the continental United States," he writes, "are not pristine and ecosystem research has shown that conditions in many are deteriorating."

Scientific study, says Allen, "strongly supports the notion that historic Euro-American use of the area has triggered unprecedented change in most of the park's ecosystems. . . . This land-use history has resulted in degraded and unsustainable conditions. . . . Similar changes have occurred throughout much of the Southwest."

Specifically, in Bandelier the soils are apparently "eroding at net rates of about one-half inch per decade. Given soil depths averaging only one to two feet in many areas, there will soon be loss of entire soil bodies across extensive areas."

This is bad "because the loss of organic topsoils, decreased plant-available water, extreme soil surface temperatures, and freeze-thaw activity impede herbaceous vegetation establishment and productivity."

Hands-off protection is not the answer. "Herbivore exclosures established in 1975 show that protection from grazing, by itself, fails to promote vegetative recovery. . . . Without management intervention, this human-induced episode of accelerated soil erosion appears to be highly persistent and irreversible. **To a significant degree, the park's biological productivity and cultural resources are literally washing away.**" [*Emphasis added.*]

According to Allen and the other authors, intervention is required in order to "reestablish functionality in the system." This will require active management and restoration, the goal of which will be "to reestablish biotic dominance over rates of erosion and enable fires to move across the landscape unimpeded."

His summation is provocative: "We have a choice when we know land is 'sick.' We can 'make believe,' to quote Aldo Leopold, that everything will turn out all right if Nature is left to take its course in our unhealthy wildernesses, or we can intervene—adaptively and with humility—to facilitate the healing process."

In a new environmentalism, "protecting" land, where it is needed at all, is only half the job.

## Restoration

The principal chore ahead of us is restoration, which I define as achieving full ecological functionality at the level of soil, grass, and water. Our job as activists, in other words, is transforming "red" to "green" on maps like that of the Altar Valley.

One does not need to be an expert in the minutiae of rangeland health to understand that we have a tremendous amount of unhealthy land out there. The catalogue is all too familiar by now—choking forests, eroding land, endangered species. Add to this list what I consider to be the most alarming trend in recent years: accelerated habitat fragmentation due to off-road vehicle damage, new road construction, and exurban development.

In light of the "functionality crisis" confronting us, renewed calls

**After:** Upper Cottonwood, June 1998. (Photo courtesy of Dave Bradford.)

for an expansion of the national wilderness system, as well as the

Erosion, pedestaling. (Photo courtesy of Kirk Gadzia.)

creation of other "protected" areas, seem anachronistic in a new century. Shielding bits of land from the threat of mechanized human activity without simultaneously confronting the source of that threat—the way we live as a society and a people—is, to paraphrase Aldo Leopold, like "improving the pump, rather than the well."

Additionally, the whole concept of "preserving" some places while "releasing" others creates a stratification of land quality and land use that is harmful to land health. For example, what about all the "Plain Jane" lands across the West not deemed worthy of "protection?" Very often, these lands are in need of ecological assistance as well. And what about the ecologically artificial distinction between public and private land (a problem exposed by the term "public lands environmen-

talism")? If the plants and animals do not recognize these boundaries, why should we?

A rangeland health paradigm, by contrast, treats all areas equally and, as a result, gives us a snapshot of functionality—a snapshot that enables land owners and managers to prioritize their restoration work, if restoration work is required. And by working at the level of soil, grass, and water, it reduces our dependence on land discrimination.

The key, I am convinced, is more stewardship, not less. By that I mean stewardship that is defined, and measured, by its effects on soil, grass, and water. Stewardship, also, that is humble.

Good stewardship also means having a full toolbox at one's disposal. This includes cattle. In fact, a whole host of new tools involving cattle have popped up recently, including grassbanks, holistic management, dormant season grazing, poop-and-stomps on mine tailings, and herding (an ancient idea that is being rediscovered).

Unfortunately, we are often precluded from using certain tools, tying our own hands, sometimes by regulation, but most often by our attitude. In his classic book, *Game Management*, Aldo Leopold wrote that wildlife "can be restored with the same tools that had hithertofore destroyed it—fire, ax, cow, gun, and plow." The difference, of course, is not the tool itself, but how we use it; and our willingness to use it in the first place.

Attitude, in other words, is as important as knowledge.

## Work

Recently, I had the privilege of riding a horse into the West Elks Wilderness, near Paonia, Colorado. I went because I wanted to see an award-winning cattle herding operation in action and learn more about the compatibility between well-managed ranching and wilderness values. I also wanted to see some pretty country.

I took two local environmental activists along, one of whom had recently backpacked the very trail we were riding. Initially, we were shocked by what we saw. The thousand-head herd had traveled the same path only a few days prior, leaving cow plops and broken vegetation everywhere. The trail had been trampled into a muddy mess. Our Forest Service guide said this was a good thing—he believed that land can tolerate, and sometimes benefit from, disturbance caused by animal impact.

I asked the backpacker, who was also the director of an active environmental organization, what she thought. "People call me all the time and complain," she said.

"They're hikers. They don't think there should be cows in the wilderness."

"What do you tell them?" I asked.

"I tell them it's a working wilderness," she replied.

And it is a wilderness that is working well by every ecological and economic indicator that I have seen.

Herdng cows in the West Elks Wilderness.

In fact, both the local Forest Service office and the pool of ranchers received national awards recently for their innovative collaboration. And they have the monitoring data to back up their claims.

But what about work? If a new environmentalism is going to do restoration, or support ecologically sensitive ranch management, it must first confront the question of human labor on the land. This is an important issue because environmentalists often deride work on public lands, equating it almost universally with destruction.

This is a problem, says historian Richard White in a provocative essay,[11] because, by segregating work from nature, environmentalists "create a set of dualisms where work can only mean the absence of nature and nature can only mean human leisure, [thus making] both humans and nonhumans. . .ultimately. . .the poorer. . . .Work once bore the burden of connecting us

> "We have a choice when we know land is 'sick.' We can 'make believe,' to quote Aldo Leopold, that everything will turn out all right if Nature is left to take its course in our unhealthy wildernesses, or we can intervene— adaptively and with humility—to facilitate the healing process."

with nature. In shifting much of this burden onto the various forms of play that take us back to nature, Americans have shifted the burden to leisure. And play cannot bear the weight."

We need to examine work, he says, or "we will condemn ourselves to spending most of our lives outside of nature, for there can be no permanent place for us inside. Having demonized those whose very lives recognize the tangled complexity of a

planet in which we kill, destroy and alter as a condition of living and working, we can claim an innocence that in the end is merely irresponsibility. . . .

"If, on the other hand," he concludes, "environmentalism could focus on our work rather than on leisure, then a whole series of fruitful new angles on the world might be possible. It links us to each other, and it links us to nature. It unites issues as diverse as workplace safety and grazing on public lands; it unites toxic sites and wilderness areas. In taking responsibility for our own lives and work, in unmasking the connections of our labor and nature's labor, in giving up our hopeless fixation on purity, we may ultimately find a way to break the borders that imprison nature as much as ourselves. Work, then, is where we should begin."

I've quoted Dr. White at length because I think his point stabs at the heart of the question about the future of the environmental movement. As I witnessed in the West Elks, and on many other ranches, work, when done responsibly and with humility, and measured by its effect on soil, grass, and water, is compatible with ecological and wilderness values. There is simply no question about it.

Wendell Berry once wrote, "The conservationist's picture of the world as either a deserted landscape or desertified landscape is too simple; it misrepresents both the world and humanity. If we are to have an

A New Environmentalism

accurate picture of the world, even in its present diseased condition, we must interpose between the unused landscape and the misused landscape a landscape that humans have used well."

However, to measure this "well-used landscape," we need to employ a new equation—one that examines the interplay between work, play, and ecology in a much more sophisticated manner than we have used in the past. One of the goals of the new environmentalism is to create a formula that allows for a more complete understanding of the sustainable aspects of the work/play/ecology dynamic.

But to accomplish this goal, we need to stop pitting one value against another.

## Good vs. Evil

A new environmentalism must avoid, at all costs, the yoke of dualisms. Good Guy vs. Bad, Work vs. Recreation, Urban vs. Rural, Wilderness vs. Wise Use, Sacred vs. Profane, Us vs. Them. In the bad ol' days of rampant clearcutting and dam-building, these dualisms served an important purpose—to call the public to arms. They remain useful today because unsustainable exploitation of our natural world still yields immense profits for a select few. But they have become a crutch, often blinding us and tying our hands.

This brings us back to the question of wilderness again. Historian William Cronon has written,

**Before**: Largo Creek, near Quemado, New Mexico, was in degraded hydrological condition. We sought advice from Bill Zeedyk (pictured).

"The critique of modernity that is one of environmentalism's most important contributions to the moral and political discourse of our time more often than not appeals, explicitly or implicitly, to wilderness as the standard against which to measure the failings of our human world."[12]

This creates a paradox in which the human exists outside the natural. "If we allow ourselves to believe that nature, to be true, must also be wild," continues Cronon, "then our very presence in nature represents its fall. The place where we are is where nature is not. If this is so—if by definition wilderness leaves no place for human beings, save perhaps as contemplative sojourners enjoying their leisurely reverie in God's natural cathedral—then also by definition it can offer no solution to the environmental and other problems that confront us."

**During:** Largo Creek, where we built simple Zeedyk structures to "induce meandering."

By indulging in a dualism that sets nature and humanity at opposite poles, we "leave ourselves little hope of discovering what an ethical, sustainable, *honorable* human place in nature might actually look like." It can also lead to environmentally irresponsible behavior.

"Our challenge is to stop thinking of such things according to a set of bipolar moral scales in which the human and the nonhuman, the natural and the unnatural, the fallen and the unfallen, serve as our conceptual map for understanding and valuing the world. Instead, we need to embrace the full continuum of a natural landscape that is also cultural, in which the city, suburb, the pastoral, and the wild each has its proper place, which we permit ourselves to celebrate without needlessly denigrating the others."

He concludes "The wilderness dualism. . .denies us the middle ground in which responsible use and non-use might attain some kind of balanced, sustainable relationship." And according to Cronon, the "middle ground is where we actually live."

I have quoted him at length because his point too is critical to the success of a new environmentalism—that we must find a way to occupy and work in the "middle ground," or what some have called the Radical Center. In my experience, work, play, soil, predators, wilderness, and agriculture can be balanced with one another—if we drop the dualisms and start shaking hands instead.

Only by working in the Radical Center will we make actual progress on the back forty.

### The Big Picture

I am not suggesting that we forgo designation of new wilderness areas or drop the tactics of confrontationalism entirely. They both serve important purposes in certain situations, though I think lawsuits are like antibiotics—great in a crisis but increasingly ineffective over time, especially as resistance builds. And a great deal of resistance has been building over the past two decades.

Furthermore, the environmental movement was forged in confrontation and adversity and will necessarily be called on again and again to fight. The trouble today, however, with a continued dependence on this form of crisis management is that it has transformed the movement into a green version of The Little Dutch Boy. Activists race around plugging holes in an increasingly leaky dike called "the environment" without significantly addressing the sources of the threat to the dike in the first place—principally, the way we live as a people.

Wendell Berry, as usual, put it best when he asked, "Can we adapt our work and our pleasure to our places so as to live in them without destroying them? Can we limit our work and our economies to a scale appropriate to our places, to our place in the order of things, and to our intelligence? Can we control ourselves?"

Or, right to the point, "Can we get beyond the assumption that it is possible to live inhumanely and yet 'save the planet' by a series of last-minute preservations of things perceived at the last minute to be endangered and, only because endangered, precious?"

A new environmentalism must address the bigger picture.

It is not enough anymore to "save" nature. We, as environmentalists, need to ask harder questions about how to work together to

**After:** Largo Creek, four months after we started working to restore it.

conserve and restore self-sustaining social and natural landscapes. We can start by addressing the *causes* of our unhealthy and unhappy world, rather than simply concentrating on the *symptoms.*

There is a parallel with the rangeland health paradigm here. By examining a watershed holistically, for instance, at the level of soil, grass, and water, we can get a good sense for causes of degradation, rather than spend our money and energy on quick technological fixes.

For example, at a public meeting I attended in Catron County a few years ago, a rancher complained about the infestation of small trees on his land by saying that "he was hardly making a dent in the forest with his backhoe." Kirk Gadzia responded by asking, not so rhetorically, "Is the problem that we don't have enough backhoes?"

Are we working on symptoms when we should be working on causes? Granted, some problems, such as global warming, may be beyond the reach of us individually, but many can be fixed at home, if we know where to look, what tools to use, and to whom to turn for assistance. All of which will require some fundamental shifts in our culture and society.

Environmentalists can help lead the way, if we want.

Cultural critic Stephanie Mills put it well when she said, "It's time to ditch the home entertainment center and break the consumer trance, time to roll up our sleeves and learn the plants. . . . We may even rescue the wildness within us from the extinction threatened by credit cards, muscle wagons, and trips to the mall. By working to restore our life places from the soil on up, we can renew our membership in the biotic community."[13]

### How It Works

I believe that the goals of a new environmentalism can be advanced by a few core strategies:

➡ **Work at the Grassroots**: Literally at the level of grass and roots. This means seeking out projects that restore watersheds one acre at a time, if need be, or reclaim mine tailings, or assist riparian areas to recover, and to do so principally by using nature's original toolbox. The objectives are to grow grass, reduce bare soil, restore conditions for fire, and a million other acts of healing.

➡ **Work Collaboratively**: Strength lies in numbers. When we argue our interests instead of our positions we often uncover acres of common ground. Practical solutions to seemingly intractable natural resource conflicts exist, but only if we are willing to work toward common goals. A rangeland health paradigm encourages collaboration by steering the discussion back to the ground, where it belongs.

➡ **Encourage Better Stewardship**: That means teaching, listening, and learning. Education is a two-way street, not a cul-de-sac with a "Do Not Enter" sign out front. Knowledge marches on, new technologies are invented, and values change. Incorporating these changes constructively means employing an open hand, not a closed fist, when dealing with ranchers and other land managers, especially those who work for the federal government.

This is an important point, given the long history of environmentalists demanding "compliance" from the federal government. I feel the need to quote Wendell Berry here again: "You can not get good care in the use of the land by demanding it from public officials. That you have the legal right to demand it does not at all improve the case. . . . The idea that a displaced people might take appropriate care of places is absurd; there is no sense in it and no hope."

➥**Lend a Hand**: The time has come to help people. The federal government can no longer carry the load of assuring proper stewardship of our public lands, because it has neither the financial, manpower, or spiritual resources to do the work alone anymore, especially as the workload expands on an almost daily basis. It is therefore incumbent on all of us to assist them somehow—bring money to the table, or monitoring services, or organize a workshop.

➥**Work Toward Results**: Measure success by progress on the back forty. Demand, and help achieve, quantifiable, real-world results. Learn how ecosystems actually operate, embrace ideas that achieve ecological and economic sustainability simultaneously, then insist that the results are monitored. Better yet, help with the monitoring **yourself**!

As I said earlier, these strategies are not theoretical; they are being implemented daily and across a wide region. What they need, however, is more support.

## Review

In summation, I believe a new environmentalism does the following:

➥Employs a rangeland health paradigm.

➥Acknowledges that the old "protection" paradigm is not terribly useful anymore.

➥Considers its principal job to be ecological and economic restoration.

➥Encourages good stewardship and values sustainable work on the land.

➥Dumps destructive dualisms.

➥Takes seriously the complex work/play/ecology equation.

➥Learns, teaches, listens, and lends a hand.

➥Achieves and monitors on-the-ground results.

➥Keeps an eye on the prize: guiding fundamental human behavior toward restraint and self-sustainability.

And one more goal:

➥Attempts to achieve what Aldo Leopold longed for so many years ago—"a state of harmony between man and land."

## References

[1] *Rangeland Health: New Methods to Classify, Inventory, and Monitor Rangelands.* National Academy of Sciences Press, Washington, D.C., 1994.

[2] *Interpreting Indicators of Rangeland Health (Technical Reference 1734-6).* Co-authored by Mike Pellant, BLM, Patrick Shaver, NRCS, David Pyke, USGS, and Jeff Herrick, ARS/ Jornada Experimental Range. USDI, Denver, 2000.

[3] *Monitoring Manual for Gassland, Shrubland and Savanna Ecosystems.* Co-developed by the USDA-ARS Jornada Experimental Range, Las Cruces, 2001.

[4] *Riparian Area Management: Process of Assessing Proper Functioning*

*Condition (TR 1737-9)*. U.S. Dept. of Interior/BLM, Washington, D.C., 1998.

[5]All Leopold quotes, unless otherwise indicated, are from *A Sand County Almanac and Sketches Here and There*. Oxford University Press, New York, 1987.

"There is a parallel with the rangeland health paradigm here. By examining a watershed holistically, for instance, at the level of soil, grass, and water, we can get a good sense for causes of degradation, rather than spend our money and energy on quick technological fixes."

[6]All Berry quotes are from *Another Turn of the Crank: Essays*. Counterpoint Press, Washington, D.C., 1995.

[7]For an in-depth analysis of the ecological underpinnings to progressive ranch management, see *The New Ranch Handbook: A Guide To Restoring Western Rangelands,* by Nathan Sayre. The Quivira Coalition, Santa Fe, 2001.

[8]In *Unmanaged Landscapes: Voices for Untamed Nature*. Edited by Bill Willers. Island Press,Washington, D.C., 1999.

[9]In *The World of Wilderness: Essays on the Power and Purpose of Wild Country*. Edited by T.H. Watkins and Patricia Byrnes. Roberts Rinehart, Niwot, Co., 1995.

[10]"Would Ecological Landscape Restoration Make the Bandelier Wilderness More or Less of a Wilderness?" by Charisse Sydoriak, Craig Allen, Brian Jacobs. In *Wild Earth*, Winter 2000/2001, pp. 83-90.

[11]"'Are You an Environmentalist or Do You Work for a Living?': Work and Nature," Richard White. In *Uncommon Ground: Rethinking the Human Place in Nature*. Edited by William Cronon. W.W. Norton, New York, 1996.

[12]"The Trouble with Wilderness; or, Getting Back to the Wrong Nature," William Cronon. In *Uncommon Ground: Rethinking the Human Place in Nature*. Edited by William Cronon. W.W. Norton, New York, 1996.

[13]In *Consuming Desires: Consumption, Culture, and the Pursuit of Happiness*. Edited by Roger Rosenblatt. Island Press, Washington, D.C., 1999.

A New Environmentalism

# Environmental Justice and Public Lands Ranching in Northern New Mexico

*by Ernest Atencio*

Ernest Atencio is a northern New Mexico native and has worked throughout the Southwest as an environmental activist, journalist, environmental educator, wilderness instructor, and park ranger. He is currently the executive director of the Valles Caldera Coalition. He spent three years as projects director for a New Mexico-based environmental advocacy organization called Amigos Bravos. His publications include a variety of environmental journalism, anthropology, natural history, reviews, essays, and creative writing. Previous professional anthropology experience includes ethnographic research and published work on western cowboy culture, Havasupai Tribe ethnohistory, and sustainable development in Ladakh, India. He also initiated and managed an oral history project for Amigos Bravos to collect and disseminate traditional local wisdom about rivers and sustainable water use in northern New Mexico. He has an M.A. in applied sociocultural anthropology from Northern Arizona University.

**Note:** *In response to a zero-grazing agenda by some members of the national Sierra Club, The Quivira Coalition and the Santa Fe Group of the Sierra Club, with support from the McCune Foundation, commissioned anthropologist and writer Ernie Atencio to prepare a report on the social, cultural, and economic consequences of ending public lands ranching in northern New Mexico. The following is a summary of that report, which has influenced national Sierra Club policy decisions. Copies of the full report are available from The Quivira Coalition. All opinions and conclusions are the author's, unless otherwise indicated.[1]*

*"History will judge greens by whether they stand with the world's poor."*—Tom Athanasiou, social ecologist[2]

## Background

In the mountains and mesas of northern New Mexico and southern Colorado, a land-based Indo-Hispano village culture persists against all odds. For over four centuries, these isolated ranching and farming communities survived the rigors of frontier life in the farthest corner of the Spanish kingdom, generations of raiding by nomadic tribes, rebellions, wars and conquest, the vagaries of weather, dispossession

---

of community lands, and desperate poverty. But they have done more than simply survive. A distinctive culture developed in the region that remains a dynamic and defining presence today. And after centuries of

> "...a zero-grazing policy would have an impact on a largely poor, Hispanic population as negative as any discriminatory environmental policy that threatens the health and welfare of disenfranchised populations of people of color in any other context."

continuity and adaptation, rural villagers have acquired a powerful sense of belonging, a rooted knowledge and reverence for their homeland, that has become rare in the modern world. "Their families have lived here for centuries; their roots are in the land; their hearts and souls are there. The tie is really mystical," explained Father Benedict Cuesta in the 1970s.[3]

Though rich in culture and history, local Hispanics have not shared in national economic prosperity throughout most of the 20th century. Even today, while the United States enjoys the strongest economic boom in its history, New Mexico remains the poorest state with the highest rate of "food insecurity" in the nation. And the north-

central counties of Mora, Río Arriba, and Taos are among the poorest in the state.[4]

Impoverished rural families have come to depend on the meager economic buffer provided by grazing a few cattle or sheep on what are now U.S. Forest Service and Bureau of Land Management lands. Perhaps the most important dimension of the story, and one that makes the northern New Mexico situation unique, is the fact that many of these "public" lands were once community land grants that have been dismantled and lost over the last 150 years through the machinations of the U.S. legal system.

It is clear from all the research, and ominously obvious to local ranchers, that ending public lands ranching here would have a devastating impact on an already strained local economy, on the social fabric of rural communities, and on the continuity of a centuries-old cultural tradition. Though not an issue that is normally considered within the realm of environmental justice, a zero-grazing policy would have an impact on a largely poor, Hispanic population as negative as any discriminatory environmental policy that threatens the health and welfare of disenfranchised populations of people of color in any other context.

Law professor Eileen Gauna frames environmental justice as "a challenge that all should be concerned about in a society that is committed to the ethical precept of basic fairness."[5] Providing support and economic and social safety nets for those less privileged has long been part of our national culture. In this context, access to public lands for grazing is the safety net that keeps some families from destitute poverty or displacement to some poor inner-city barrio.

This report is not intended as an apology or excuse for those who abuse public lands or pad their profits at the public's expense. There is no argument that irresponsible livestock grazing can have a nega-tive impact, especially in this arid region, on important ecological processes, on erosion, on natural vegetational succession, on watershed health and productivity. There is no argument that some ranchers have not demon-strated much success with sustainable management in the past. Serious problems exist, and they have to be dealt with. On the other hand, it's important to recognize the fact that ranchers clearly have a vested interest in conservation and sustainability, and many take their stewardship very seriously.

I will sidestep those issues, not because they are irrelevant or unimportant, but because they are being very successfully addressed through many other avenues. But I will say that there is strong and growing evidence that conscientious grazing practices and new approaches to holistic range management, in the right places, at the right times, can be

El Valle. Overlook from the uplands, showing river valley farming and the rural village of Sena. (Photo courtesy of Crystal.)

genuinely sustainable and even enhance natural habitat and biodiversity (contact The Quivira Coalition for more information).[6]

## Environmental Justice

During the last decade of the 20th century, the environmental movement was forced to recognize the fact that people of color and the poor have been left out of the dia-logue about environmental issues and often fall through the cracks of environmental regulations.[7] While we were busy worrying about the pressing problems of dwindling wildlands; dammed, over-appropriated and polluted rivers; and biodiversity, poor people got poorer and continued to bear the brunt of toxic industry. Certain environmental groups, including the Sierra Club,

> "Public health impacts from environmental conditions or hazardous waste, or discrimination in the implementation and enforcement of environmental policies, are unquestionably critical problems, but environmental justice is about more than that. It is also about widening the discourse on environmental issues to include the perspectives, values, and concerns of the traditionally ignored populations of people of color and the poor."

responded commendably by broadening their approach to at least consider environmental justice issues. But some people and some issues continue to fall through the cracks.

Public health impacts from environmental conditions or hazardous waste, or discrimination in the implementation and enforcement of environmental policies, are unquestionably critical problems, but environmental justice is about more than that. It is also about widening the discourse on environmental issues to include the perspectives, values, and concerns of the tradition-

ally ignored populations of people of color and the poor.

In 1992, then Sierra Club Executive Director Michael Fischer called for "a friendly takeover of the Sierra Club by people of color," and optimistically declared that "the struggle for environmental justice in this country and around the globe must be a primary goal of the Sierra Club during its second century."[8]

An anthropologist at a recent conference I attended suggested that there will soon be no nature to protect, unless we address social justice issues to share the world's resources more equitably.[9] Protecting natural ecosystems will become a moot point, in other words, if the poor of the world continue to be left farther and farther behind, struggling for their slice of a shrinking pie of natural resources. As one person put it, "In the metaphor of a rapidly sinking ship, we are all in the same boat, and the people of color are closest to the hole."[10]

Environmental justice is not whole, then, unless it recognizes the inescapable global forces of political economy that perpetuate cycles of poverty and environmental abuses, and unless it addresses social and economic justice as integral components.

Despite many ongoing efforts in northern New Mexico, bridging those persistent gaps between environmental, social, and economic concerns is still a challenge. It straddles and obscures comfortable categories and tests the limits of the more strident and dogmatic on both sides of the proverbial fence. For lack of a handy category, this perplexing hybrid activism is even occasionally, and inaccurately, lumped together with the anti-environmental "wise use" movement.

Rancher and professional range manager Virgil Trujillo says it well. "The environmental movement has been excellent in the sense that it makes us aware of our environment. But we've got to stop the nonsense of wasting all those resources, attacking each other, yelling at each other. Turn the situation around and let's start yelling for each other, for each other's health, so to speak."[11]

## Findings

While the abject poverty and economic crisis that spawned the New Deal era of the 1930s may be ancient history to most Americans, northern New Mexico still carries that legacy. Any way you spin the statistics, New Mexico ranks as the poorest state, the three northern counties of Mora, Río Arriba, and Taos are even poorer, and the local Hispanic population is among the poorest of the poor. All socioeconomic indicators paint a consistent

Virgil Trujillo. (All photos courtesy of Courtney White, unless otherwise indicated.)

picture of chronic poverty and limited access to education and other opportunities. In this context, most local ranchers are just scraping by, supplementing meager incomes from other jobs with the little economic buffer provided by grazing a few cattle on public land.

Northern New Mexico cattle ranching is a small-scale enterprise. The average size of a grazing permit on the Santa Fé National Forest, for instance, is 41 cattle. Only 8% of all permits on the forest are for herds anywhere near a commercial scale of 100 or more.[12] With the characteristic small operations in this struggling economy, profit margins from ranching are slim to none. Instead, local Hispanic ranchers often view their livestock as "banks-on-the-hoof" that can be tapped in hard times, used as a backup for emergencies, used to cover unpredictable periods of unemployment, or to pay college tuition for their kids. Basic subsistence by way of meat and milk are an important part of that bank

Cleveland mill.

account for most families.[13]

"That's kaput," says Aparcio Gurulé about the impact to his family ranching operation of ending public lands grazing.[14] A 1994 study found that if public lands ranching were shut down, 56% of those surveyed in New Mexico would continue to operate, but on a smaller scale, and 44% would not.[15] In a strapped economy, realistic alternatives are few and far between.

Cattle ranching in northern New Mexico may in fact not be economically viable in a purist economic analysis. But the danger of straight and narrow economic thinking is that it fails to take into account the less quantifiable, though

no less important, issues of social well being and cultural vitality. A conventional economic view also usually fails to take into account other tangible but indirect consequences of straight economic decisions. Local, small-scale ranching may not seem a worthy pursuit in our modern, technology-based, runaway economy, but exchanging a rural economic struggle for an urban one, or pushing rural villagers closer to poverty and welfare, clearly makes no sense economically or socially.

Responsibility and respect toward the environment is expressed in numerous and well-documented traditional land-use practices, cultural values and customs, sayings or *dichos*, and oral history comprising parables of the ethics and morality of caring for the land.[16] No culture on the planet can claim a history of perfect, sustainable natural resource stewardship. Nonetheless, an ethos of restraint is and has been the general guiding principle of resource use, or "cultural ecology," in northern New Mexico for centuries.

A history of astonishing injustice surrounding the loss of communal land grants is a prevalent theme among local villagers, and particularly relevant to questions about public lands. In a nutshell,

An Invitation to the Radical Center

"The establishment of national forests in New Mexico also resulted in the abrogation of Spanish-American property rights. Much of the land now included in the National Forest System in northern New Mexico was once part of the many Spanish and Mexican land grants in the region. The inhabitants of the numerous Spanish-American mountain villages located their settlements in valleys and along streams wherever valley floors were large enough for village sites and irrigated farm plots. The forested mountains, usually part of the village communal lands or *ejidos*, were used for grazing, hunting, fishing, and obtaining firewood. . . . When the Forest Service acquired these lands, these use rights were not acknowledged. The loss of grazing lands and the resources of the mountain forests brought poverty to a large number of Spanish-American village people."[17]

Beyond the extensive literature about the long history and the social, cultural, and economic importance of ranching in this area, it's also important to hear directly from the people who still do it and who would be most directly affected by shutting down public lands ranching. Along with the other research, I interviewed six northern New Mexico ranchers who rely on federal public lands grazing for some

portion of their livelihood, and their voices are found throughout the report. They include Ricardo Fresquez of Mora; Aparcio Gurulé, a full-time ranchero from Cuba; George Maestas and Andie Sanchez of the Santa Barbara Grazing Association; rancher and economist Joe Torres of the Valle Vidal Grazing Association; and Virgil Trujillo, ranch manager at Ghost Ranch and

George Maestas speaking to a workshop at the Peñasco High School.

board member of The Quivira Coalition.

These are not people with a narrow anti-environmental, pro-industry agenda. The world is not that black and white in northern New Mexico. They are just reasonable men who care about the land, their communities, and their culture, who are simply trying to make a living like everyone else. Here is some of what they have to say.

In a common lament, George Maestas says that there is a "presumption that traditional users have ruined or will ruin these public lands. In general, our riparian areas and forests are relatively healthy." Policy and management decisions that affect ecological health are out of local ranchers' hands, he says. "To

Overgrown forests of northern New Mexico.

the extent that our forests' health has deteriorated, it can largely be attributed to management policies that have been mandated and imposed on us. Policies like indiscriminate fire suppression, and prohibitions on timber and firewood removal have left our forests overgrown with little forage for our cattle or wildlife and susceptible to catastrophic fire."[18]

Another common lament, and something that mystifies local villagers, is the way the national environmental agenda often lumps together local, small-scale, potentially sustainable resource use with multi-national, profit-driven, industrial-

scale exploitation. As Aparcio Gurulé says, "Don't compare them with Ted Turner and those big kids, you know?"

About policy issues that deal with biodiversity, Virgil Trujillo says, "Well, I think the endangered species protection is critical, but while we get narrow-minded and focused down on an individual species, again—and keep forgetting about how the whole picture sticks together—that then causes a big concern for me. If we're losing our watersheds also to this tree encroachment, and so on and so forth. If it's affecting the way our rivers run and so on and so forth, it concerns me when we focus and narrow-mind ourselves down to one little issue and spend millions of dollars on it, instead of standing back and looking at the big picture. . . . It's a complicated issue. I share my environment with all the creatures. All have equal right."

**Conclusion**

With threats to the natural resource-based rural economy, dark visions of wholesale resort development or subdivisions are not far-fetched in this area fast being discovered, and gentrified, by well-heeled immigrants from the cities. But this is more than a "cows vs. condos" argument. And it is more than an argument of cows vs. the loss of mere lifestyle or profession choice. It is an argument of cows vs. the loss of a unique culture and society that have endured in this region for 400 years.

Without access to public lands, it's clear that an age-old tradition, and an essential local economic pursuit, would probably be over. Losing legal title to community land grants is one thing, but losing all access to centuries-old traditional grazing lands would be the final blow. Not only would the rich fabric of social, cultural, and economic continuity begin to fray, but local ranchers who are barely staying afloat as it is in a floundering local economy would find themselves in worse condition, struggling to provide even the basic comforts, food, and education for their families. It would be yet another in the long legacy of injustices to impoverished Hispanic villagers.

## Footnotes

[1] Ernie is currently working on a report on logging issues and environmental justice in northern New Mexico.

[2] Athanasiou 1998, p.304. The more complete quote in context reads: "Given the key role they are fated to play in the politics of an ever-shrinking world, it is past time for environmentalists to face their own history, in which they have too often stood not for justice and freedom, or even for realism, but merely for the comforts and aesthetics of

affluent nature lovers. They have no choice. History will judge greens by whether they stand with the world's poor."

[3] Quoted in Carlson 1990, p. 109.

[4] Nord, Jemison, and Bickel 1999; Census 1993; Census 2000.

[5] E. Guana 2000.

[6] See Dagget and Dusard 1998; The Quivira Coalition n.d.

"To the extent that our forests' health has deteriorated, it can largely be attributed to management policies that have been mandated and imposed on us. Policies like indiscriminate fire suppression, and prohibitions on timber and firewood removal have left our forests overgrown with little forage for our cattle or wildlife and susceptible to catastrophic fire."—George Maestas

[7] The now legendary letter from economic and social justice activists to the "Group of Ten" national environmental organizations in 1990 is what brought national attention to the environmental justice movement. See Sierra Club 1993; SWOP 1990.

[8] Sierra Club 1993, p. 51.

[9] Pramod Parajuli, speaking on "Endangered Peoples" at the 1999 meeting of the Society for Applied Anthropology, "Constructing Common Ground: Human and Environmental Imperatives."

[10]Deeohn Ferris, September 1991, quoted in J. Guana 2000, p. 6.

[11]From an interview at Ghost Ranch on August 8, 2000.

[12]Raw numbers for cattle permits, with cattle per permittee, from Sylvia Valdez of the Santa Fé National Forest, August 2, 2000.

Chimayo.

[13]Eastman and Gray 1987; Eastman, Raish, and McSweeney 2000.

[14]From an interview in Cuba on August 9, 2000.

[15]Fowler, J.M. *et al*, 1994, *Economic Characteristics of the Western Livestock Industry*, cited in Eastman, Raish, and McSweeney 2000, p. 542.

[16]Arellano 1997; Atencio 1987; Nostrand 1992; Peña 1998; Peña and Martinez 1998, van Dresser 1972; Van Ness 1987.

[17]Knowlton 1970, pp. 1070-1071.

[18]From a letter to the author dated August 26, 2000.

## Selected Bibliography

Arellano, Juan Estévan. "La Querencia: La Raza Bioregionalism." *New Mexico Historical Review*, January 1997, pp. 31-37.

Atencio, Tomás. "Cultural Philosophy: A Common Sense Perspective." In *Upper Río Grande Waters— Strategies: A Conference on Traditional Water Use.* The Upper Río Grande Working Group, ed. Albuquerque: Southwest Hispanic Research Institute and Native American Studies Center, 1987.

Athanasiou, Tom. *Divided Planet: The Ecology of Rich and Poor.* Athens: University of Georgia Press, 1998.

Bureau of the Census (Census). 1990 *Census of Population and Housing: Population and Housing Characteristics for Census Tracts and Block Numbering Areas, New Mexico (Outside Metropolitan Areas).* Washington: U.S. Department of Commerce Bureau of the Census, 1993.

*2000 U.S. Census*, U.S. Department of Commerce. Electronic document. http//www.census.gov.

Carlson, Alvar W. *The Spanish American Homeland: Four Centuries in New Mexico's Río Arriba.* Baltimore: Johns Hopkins University Press, 1990.

Dagget, Dan and Jay Dusard. *Beyond the Rangeland Conflict: Toward a West that Works.* Flagstaff, AZ: Good Stewards Project, 1998.

Eastman, Clyde and James R. Gray. *Community Grazing: Practice and*

*Potential in New Mexico.* Albuquerque: University of New Mexico Press, 1987.

Eastman, Clyde, Carol Raish, and Alice McSweeney. "Small livestock operations in northern New Mexico." In *Livestock Management in the American Southwest: Ecology, Society, and Economics.* Roy Jemison and Carol Raish, eds. Pp. 523-554. New York: Elsevier, 2000.

Gauna, Eileen. "Environmental Justice: The Big View." *Green Fire Report* (New Mexico Environmental Law Center Newsletter) Special Issue, Fall/Winter 1999-2000, pp. 2-4.

Gauna, Jeanne. "Environmental Injustice in New Mexico." *Green Fire Report* (New Mexico Environmental Law Center Newsletter) Special Issue, Fall/Winter 1999-2000, pp. 5-6.

Knowlton, Clark S. "Violence in New Mexico: A Sociological Perspective." *California Law Review* 1970, vol. 58, no. 4, pp.1054-1085.

Nord, Mark, Kyle Jemison, and Gary Bickel. *Measuring Food Security in the United States: Prevalence of Food Insecurity and Hunger, by State, 1996-1998.* Food Assistance and Nutrition Research Report Number 2. Washington: U.S. Department of Agriculture Economic Research Service 1999.

Nostrand, Richard L. *The Hispano Homeland.* Norman: University of Oklahoma Press, 1992.

Peña, Devon G., ed. "Los Animalitos: Culture, Ecology, and the Politics of Place in the Upper Río Grande." In *Chicano Culture, Ecology, Politics: Subversive Kin.* Pp. 25-57. Tucson: University of Arizona Press, 1998.

Peña, Devon G. and Rubén O. Martinez. "The Capitalist Tool, the Lawless, the Violent: A Critique of Recent Southwestern Environmental History." In *Chicano Culture, Ecology,*

*Politics: Subversive Kin.* Devon G. Peña, ed. Pp. 141-176. Tucson: University of Arizona Press, 1998.

Quivira Coalition. n.d. Quarterly Newsletters. The Quivira Coalition, June 1997-August 2000.

Sierra Club. "A Place at the Table: A Sierra Club Roundtable on Race, Justice, and the Environment." *Sierra* May/June 1993, pp. 51-58, 90-91.

SouthWest Organizing Project (SWOP). Letter to the "Group of Ten" national environmental organizations callng for an open dialogue to integrate concerns of people of color into the national environmental agenda. From Richard Moore and Jeanne Gauna, Co-Directors of the SWOP in Albuquerque, and 103 other signatories, March 16, 1990.

van Dresser, Peter. *A Landscape for Humans: A Case Study of the Potentials for Ecologically Guided Development in an Uplands Region.* Albuquerque: Biotechnic Press, 1972.

Van Ness, John R. "Hispanic Land Grants: Ecology and Subsistence in the Uplands of Northern New Mexico and Southern Colorado." In *Land, Water, and Culture: New Perspectives on Hispanic Land Grants.* Charles L. Briggs and John R. Van Ness, eds. Pp. 141-214. Albuquerque: University of New Mexico Press, 1987.

# It's the Watershed, Stupid

*by Sid Goodloe*

Sid Goodloe began his work in New Mexico land stewardship and education some 47 years ago. In purchasing Carrizo Valley Ranch in southeast New Mexico, he found the perfect mix—a worn-out, ecologically abused ranch (i.e., affordable); a location amenable to the use of multiple resources (i.e., to make ends meet); an indication of a landscape previously including running water (petroglyphs); and a wonderful place to raise his growing family. Because he recognized the need to make use of a variety of resources in order to be able to operate a cattle ranch, Sid soon made choices that resulted in:

• a new breed of cattle better suited to the environment (Alpine Black);

•a range management system that included thinning of invasive vegetative species (piñon, juniper, and pine thickets), making use of the material in firewood and viga sales (to finance rehabilitation work);

•the first use of high-intensity, short-duration grazing in the U.S.; and

•overall improvement of habitat and watershed throughout the ranch. His education at Texas A&M encouraged his natural inclination to try new things. As he gained knowledge and experience by working abroad, he invested it by putting it to work on the Carrizo Valley Ranch. Today, the ranch is the beneficiary of Sid's experiences working with agriculturalists as varied as the "old time" cowboys of Texas, the Massai, Allan Savory, R.O. Anderson, and the Gauchos of Brazil. Sid restored his degraded riparian area by first letting it rest, and then by grazing it only in the dormant season. His success, and his concern for healthy riparian areas in the state, led him to found the New Mexico Riparian Council. He has been a champion of riparian recovery ever since. Sid believes strongly in the need for sustainable agriculture and open space. He established the Southern Rockies Agricultural Land Trust to assist ranchers in placing conservation easements on their land.

When the word "riparian" became a buzzword, I had no idea what people were referring to. After I looked it up, I was still pretty much in the dark until it finally dawned on me that I was actually bringing back a "riparian area" here on the Carrizo Valley Ranch without knowing it had a sophisticated name.

I had become aware that something was drastically wrong with this ranch. (I could have used the word "ecosystem" here, but I didn't know what that meant either.) The canyons and draws had straight cut sides with nothing in the bottom but boulders. When it rained, you could almost walk on the run-off because it carried so much silt. It didn't take a lot of scientific research to come to the conclusion that something upstream was terribly wrong.

I began to notice how young and close together the piñon, juniper, and ponderosa trees were, and how little herbaceous growth occurred under them to hold the soil. Sheet erosion was moving a lot of that topsoil and accelerating water flow. Gullies were prominent, and all of this led to scoured-out canyons and draws at the lower elevations of the watershed.

## "Time-controlled grazing and piñon-juniper control have been the back-bone of my management here on Carrizo Valley Ranch...."

### What Was It Like Before?

I knew this was not the way the "ecosystem" should function. What was it like before settlement, and why did a thundershower turn these canyons and draws into a rock-rolling torrent of muddy water? Like most newcomers to New Mexico, I thought those piñon-juniper thickets belonged here. How could they be the cause of this silt-laden runoff? I thought trees stopped erosion. Was Carrizo Canyon actually at one time a meandering stream and riparian area?

The answer came one day when I was looking at some 500-year-old petroglyphs nearby. Among the rain gods, deer, and turkey were fish and beaver chiseled into the rock. How could fish live in this environment, and what self-respecting beaver would try to build a dam of cactus and alligator juniper? After perusing some 1880 surveyor's notes that indicated open grassland where now there was a solid canopy of invading trees, I came to the conclusion that something had to be done and quickly.

A little historical research made me aware of the number of livestock that had used this country, not only after the Civil War, but as far back as 1590, when the Spanish introduced sheep, cattle, and goats into the Southwest. The large increase in cattle numbers came after 1870. At that time, we had 4.5 million head in the 17 western states. By 1884, the cattle population had exploded to 47 million. Year-long grazing by these excessive numbers of cattle, followed by increasingly efficient fire suppression, had provided optimum conditions for piñon, juniper, ponderosa, and sagebrush. These plants were not only out-competing the grass, but were demanding so much more water that the aquifers were no longer producing permanent water flow that could sustain riparian conditions.

### "Watershed Restoration"

I guess you could call what began here on Carrizo Valley Ranch over 30 years ago "watershed restoration." Our initial move was to attack the water-hungry invaders that were causing the problem. Once the brush had been thinned to pre-settlement levels, and a grass cover re-established, runoff was reduced to the point that I could now concentrate on healing the scoured-out canyons and draws. If beaver and fish had lived there before, what should I do to rehabilitate these areas now that the watershed was becoming more productive? I decided that since livestock are a lot like people—when it's hot and dry, or just dry, they like to stay around a cool place where there's something appetizing to eat and plenty to drink—perhaps I needed to change their grazing patterns.

I had noticed that the lower part of the ranch, where I had deferred grazing during the summers, had begun to grow vegetation and collect silt in the canyon bottoms. It was about that time that the word "riparian" began to appear in articles about public land grazing and in conservation magazines.

## Responding Rapidly

These areas that were rested during most of the growing season and grazed during the dormant season were responding much more rapidly than I believed possible. Now that the watershed was functioning properly, I had water even in the driest part of the summer. It sup-

ported all that new vegetation that was becoming established in what was now an authentic riparian zone. Forage production was so much greater there than anywhere else on the ranch that I decided to improve

Sid's restored riparian area. (All photos courtesy of Sid Goodloe.)

on that situation anywhere I could. There were some areas that could be deferred only by fencing. Once I bit the bullet and built the fences, the response was, again, much greater than I expected.

There are many side benefits to a sustainable riparian area—one being the elimination of the need to chop ice in cold weather, because now there is a running stream where before a dry, scoured-out canyon existed. During the snowstorms of late December here in Lincoln County, it would have been very difficult to provide water to my cattle for several days had I not had ice-free running water in my riparian areas.

In addition to a dependable water supply, willows and other riparian vegetation provide feed for livestock and wildlife even in deep snow. Growth and reproduction of these

Sid's Alpine Black cows.

plants are stimulated by grazing or browsing during the dormant season.

## Rewards

I have been rewarded both aesthetically and financially for riparian rehabilitation. Intermittent ponds in the riparian area have fish and waterfowl and attract wildlife to the point that sometimes I wonder if I am going to have to exclude them also. So far no excessive damage has occurred, and my family and I enjoy the view as well as the income from fee-hunting.

Time-controlled grazing and piñon-juniper control have been the backbone of my management here on Carrizo Valley Ranch since that time. Using these management tools and a large helping of prescribed fire, the watershed above the Carrizo riparian area has been returned to pre-settlement vegetation (savannah and open woodland). Without this essential watershed rehabilitation and maintenance, the riparian area below would not be sustainable in years of sparse precipitation.

Now, with public attention focused on the less than 3% of our rangeland that is classified as riparian, I try to convey the broader aspect of the entire ecosystem and I say to them "No, no—it's the WATERSHED."

Contrast between Sid Goodloe's ranch on the right and Forest Service land on the left, which shows the encroachment of piñon-juniper on the untreated public land.

# What About Nature?
## Or What Does Nature Have to Say About Grazing?
*by Dan Dagget*

**D**an Dagget is an environmentalist and author of *Beyond the Rangeland Conflict,* on the subject of applying collaborative solutions to Western ecosystems—a publication that has been described as one of the most important books on the contemporary West. In 1992, the Sierra Club, as part of its centennial celebration, honored Dagget as one of the top 100 grassroots environmental activists in America. He has given more than 100 talks around the West on the outstanding results that environmentalists and ranchers achieve when they apply a results-based approach and work together. Currently, he contributes articles to *Range Magazine, High Country News' Writers on the Range,* and The Quivira Coalition's newsletter, among others.

A friend of mine who teaches ecosystem studies at Northern Arizona University regularly takes his students out onto nearby rangelands for field trips. When he does, he usually asks them whether the lands they're visiting are healthy or not. Often, he says, the students have trouble answering. They fidget and get nervous and eventually ask him a question: "Is this land grazed or not?"

Many of us would experience the same unease if we were put in the middle of black grama grass, rabbit-brush, and juniper in which we couldn't see any obvious clues as to how it was being managed. And so we would likely ask the same question my friend's students ask: "Is this land grazed or not?"

And if the answer we get is "Yes," most likely we would respond as those students do. We would say the land was unhealthy. If, on the other hand, we were told, "No, this land isn't being grazed," most of us would say the land was healthy no matter what it looked like.

We would answer in that way because most of us assume that if land is being left alone it is healthy. In fact, that's what most of us mean by healthy when it comes to the land—that it is being left alone. We're like an environmentalist I know who was talking to a rancher one day when the rancher offered: "Tell me what you want this land to be, and I'll make that my goal and manage toward it, and then we can be allies instead of adversaries."

The environmentalist thought a while and then answered, "There's only one thing you can do to make this place better. . .you can leave. Because if you leave, whatever happens will be natural, and therefore good, and if you stay, whatever happens will be artificial, and therefore bad."

There's a problem with this approach to judging the health of rangeland ecosystems. For one thing, using this technique, we can judge whether a piece of land is healthy or not without even seeing it.

If you don't think this sort of judging can get you into trouble, I've got some examples that might change your mind. Some of them you've already read about in issues of The Quivira Coalition newsletter. Some of them you haven't.

### U Bar Ranch

First, consider David Ogilvie's U Bar Ranch along the Gila River in southwestern New Mexico

(see "The Southwestern Willow Flycatcher and Me," pp. 27-32). This ranch, at present, serves as the home to more endangered Southwestern Willow Flycatchers than any other place in the world. The reason those birds are there, scientists tell us, is because of the way David manages his ranch. Specifically, because he has returned water flow to a series of dirt irrigation ditches whose natural leakage nurtures a riparian forest of cottonwoods and box elders that serves as habitat for the Flycatchers. David's management includes grazing cattle in some areas where the Flycatchers are nesting and feeding. If you would say the land is unhealthy because cattle graze there, you may want to clear that with the Flycatchers. They, obviously, have endorsed David Ogilvie's management with their presence, with their nests, and with the highest rate of breeding success of any known population. Southwestern Willow Flycatchers, in other words, would say that, as far as they're concerned, this is some of the healthiest land on the planet.

### Cyprus Miami Copper Mine

Next, consider an area where Terry Wheeler, a rancher and ecologist from Globe, Arizona, has used cattle to initiate natural healing processes to transform an ecological disaster into a green and growing grassland.

The restoration site is located on a pile of copper mine tailings roughly 1,100 acres in area and up to

[Top] David Ogilvie, Scott Stoleson of the Rocky Mountain Research Station, and others on the U Bar's Southwestern Willow Flycatcher habitat. (Photo courtesy of Courtney White.) [Bottom] The Southwestern Willow Flycatcher feeds its young on the U Bar Ranch. (Photo courtesy of Jean-Luc Cartron.)

300 feet thick at the Cyprus Miami Copper Mine in Miami, Arizona, southeast of Phoenix. These tailing are what's left of copper-bearing rock that has been dug up, crushed to the consistency of talcum powder, and then treated with a combination of chemical agents which includes, among other things, cyanide. After the chemicals have been used to leach the copper and other marketable minerals from the ore, the leftover slurry is drained and piped onto the huge intentional spill I have just described. There the tailings sit in suspended animation, a dilemma Nature has been unable to solve, incorporate, or re-claim for more than half a century.

Terry, who grew up in Globe, looked at that pile of mine tailings for most of his life and saw nothing but sterile rock dust and the prob-lems it caused. After taking a course in Holistic Management, however, he saw the same area as an opportunity and a challenge. "That course got me to thinking," Wheeler declared. "Soil's a living thing. It's made up of rock dust and micro-organisms. We've got plenty of rock dust. All we need is to add the micro-organisms."

Wheeler surmised that, by enriching the tailings with organic material in the form of hay and by having cattle trample that hay into the tailings and add the microbes from their gut to jumpstart the process of decay, which is the essence of a living soil, he could turn that sterile pile of mine tailings into a living ecosystem.

And so he did. After a lot of hard work and sweat and wondering

The Cyprus Miami Copper Mine, before reclamation. (Photo courtesy of Dan Dagget.)

whether this method was going to work or not, Terry Wheeler and the cows he calls Four-Legged Organic Soil Builders (or "FLOSBees") covered a considerable chunk of that tailings pile with green growing grass, and they were making steady head-way on the rest.

So, here you are on a field trip, like those students, getting ready to answer the question, Is this land healthy or not? First, you walk out onto the untreated tailings. As you do, you sink in almost to your shoe tops. When cattle step onto this stuff, they sink in sometimes to their chests. As you look around, you notice that the only things growing here are a few small, spindly weeds, and they're crusted with tailings. A puff of wind gusts past you and propels a mare's tail of dust into the

The Cyprus Mine, after reclamation. (Photo courtesy of Dan Dagget.)

air and down into the town of Miami. In the restaurants there, they joke about eating "tailings tacos."

Next, you walk out onto the part of the waste pile on which Terry Wheeler and his cows have restarted the natural ecosystem processes associated with functioning grasslands. Here, grass reaches to your knees, in some places higher. You notice that it's cooler here, too, and that the wind's not as strong because the plants diffuse the heat rays and break up the wind currents. When you look down, you notice that there is still plenty of bare dirt between the plants, but in these areas you see a thick thatch of hay trampled into the soil, armoring it against erosion. As you look closer, you see deer droppings and then the droppings of

other animals. There were no such signs of life over on the untreated tailings.

If I were to ask you which of these two places is healthiest, the grazed or the ungrazed one, what would you say? If you have any trouble answering at all, consider what the plants have said. What have the deer said? What does the wind say? Have they said land is automatically unhealthy if it's grazed?

## 60 Years of Rest

Not too far from Terry Wheeler's mine tailings restoration, a barbed-wire fence separates a ten-acre watershed study plot from the surrounding desert rangeland. A sign inside the exclosure indicates that the land within the fence has been protected from livestock grazing since 1934—more than 60 years. The land outside the exclosure has continued to be grazed by cattle for those same 60+ years.

The startling thing about this living comparison is that both sides of the fence are virtually the same. More than 60 years of protection has produced no more diversity, no more grass, no more wildlife on the protected side than on the unprotected side. And on the unprotected or grazed side, more than 60 years of continued use, or as some would call it, abuse, has produced no less vegetation and wildlife and no more bare ground than on the "protected" side. This plot is not some oddball anomaly. Hundreds, maybe thousands, of similar comparisons exist all over the West. Of the scores I have seen, all have been just as unsupportive of the absolutist assumptions most of us make when we learn that a piece of land has been grazed or not.

## What Is Nature Telling Us?

Consider what Nature is telling us in the places I've just described. When we do something that affects the environment (which is almost everything we do), the language which Nature uses to tell us whether it works or not is results.

Actions directed toward Nature are questions—"Does this work?" "If we do this, do we get what we want?"

Results are the answers. Bare dirt is an answer. So are two places that are identical in spite of the fact that they are being managed in ways most of us see as the antithesis of one another. In this case, the answer is: "No difference."

When we pay attention to those answers, we engage in a functional conversation with Nature—a dialogue. When we don't pay attention, we make what Nature has to say irrelevant in the same way we make

what anyone says irrelevant when we ask a question and don't listen to their reply.

By giving us a riparian forest full of proliferating Flycatchers, and

Another of Terry Wheeler's mine reclamation projects using cattle, in Globe, Arizona. (Photo courtesy of Dan Dagget.)

by growing grass in an area where all other efforts to grow it have failed, it seems to me that Nature has said, "Yes, this works," with regard to what Terry Wheeler and David Ogilvie have done. By giving pioneers like these the remarkable results they have achieved, it seems clear that Nature has said in no uncertain terms that it is illegitimate to assume that if land is grazed, then it must be unhealthy.

Getting back to that fence that's grazed on one side and not on the other—by giving us the same results on both sides of that fence, Nature seems to be saying that it is also illegitimate to assume that land that's not grazed is always healthier than similar land that is. And, since that fence line comparison is only a few miles from the place where Terry Wheeler has used grazing to jumpstart the natural processes which create and sustain a functioning grassland, it would seem that Nature is telling us that protection is not even more "natural" than grazing. In fact, in some cases it is less so.

The Quivira Coalition is currently engaged in a number of results-based dialogues with Nature around New Mexico. At present, we're just asking questions, which means we're taking action. And while we're at it, we're monitoring closely to make sure we don't miss any of Nature's replies.

# Science
# in the Radical Center

Forging a West that Works:

Forging a West that Works:

Forging a West that Works:

Forging a West that Works:

94

# Melding Rangeland Ecology and Livestock Management

*by Kris Havstad*

Kris Havstad is the supervisory scientist for the U.S. Department of Agriculture's Agricultural Research Service Arid Rangeland Reserach Unit based at the Jornada Experimental Range in Las Cruces, New Mexico. He has held this position since 1989. Prior to this position, he spent eight years on the faculty in the Department of Animal and Range Sciences at Montana State University in Bozeman, Montana.

## Introduction

Over 60 years ago, F. E. Mollin wrote an article entitled *If and when it rains: the stockman's view of the range question,* published by the American National Live Stock Association (1938). That article conveyed the idea that our western rangelands were in good shape and any deteriorated lands would be restored with adequate rain. We've come a long way from the extremism of that 1930s dust bowl perspective. We now know that many of our western rangelands have been overgrazed, that some areas remain in degraded states despite adequate rainfall, and that some rangelands shouldn't be grazed by livestock. Yet, we also know fairly clearly that livestock grazing of rangelands can be a sustainable practice for many sites,

for many seasons, and for many years. Extensive experimentation has illustrated that grazing can be managed and the integrity of rangeland ecosystems, in terms of their ability to produce, capture, and store nutrients and to conserve soil resources, can be maintained.

The purpose of this essay is to outline a scientific perspective that links rangeland ecology with management of rangeland grazing by livestock. We know that well-managed grazing on appropriate sites is characterized by managerial control over the intensity, timing, and frequency of livestock grazing. We also know that some sites may require periods of rest and/or very controlled grazing management practices. Irrespective, the livestock management principles underlying

---

these practices have been well described and don't need elaboration in this essay. What needs elaboration are the ecological intricacies of these rangelands, and the ecological processes that should be the basis for their management.

Fenceline contrast on David Ogilvie's Ranch. The pasture on the left is 100 acres in size and carried 275 head of livestock for one week. The pasture on the right is 1,500 acres; it supported the same herd for four weeks. Grazing pressure was therefore much greater in the left pasture. The difference is timing: the left pasture has had a growing season to recover, while the right pasture has not. (Photo courtesy of Nathan Sayre.)

## Understanding and Modification

During the 20th century, we witnessed tremendous advancements in our knowledge of ourselves as organisms. Our understandings of our anatomy, our physiology, our nutritional requirements, the clinical basis for evaluating our psyche, our reproductive functions and behaviors, and our intellectual capacity are truly startling. This knowledge is from whole organism to sub-cellular, and from conception to death. Yet, we still are faced with significant gaps in our knowledge of critical elements influencing our individual survival, such as cures for certain diseases, variable consequences of aging, intricacies of our genetic code, and environmental influences on emotional development.

For example, there is no clear scientific basis supporting a specific "blueprint" for a parent to follow in rearing a child. Certainly, there are basic ethical beliefs for a particular culture within our society that might guide child rearing. However, a single methodology derived from hypothesis-based scientific experimentation and that services all possible combinations of parents, children, and environments does not exist. The science-based knowledge we have today provides the opportunity to raise healthy, well-educated children with longer life spans. Yet, how we accomplish that is still subject to debate, trial and error, opinion, prior experiences, outside influences, sudden disruptions, changing environments, cultural traditions, community mores, and individual characteristics.

Like the human sciences, we have an impressive knowledge base about specific processes that occur within ecosystems where we live. We understand many basic elements of nutrient cycling, primary production, and soil genesis, for example. This understanding has been rapid given that studies about nature and our environment are relatively recent. (The term "ecosystem" was not defined until the 20th century.) Yet, like human nature, there does not exist a single science-based blueprint for how we interact with our environment. The actual definition of ecology is the study of how organisms interact with their environment. Most of us are probably at least amateur ecologists in that we, at a minimum, try to understand and learn about our interactions with our environment. There are certainly some elements of ethical belief that permeate our understandings and shape our basic principles guiding our interactions with our environment. However, environmental management is constrained by our ability to manipulate only a few components of a landscape.

## Thousands of Variables

It is difficult for us to manage growth and development of ourselves, our families, and our communities, and management of arid and semiarid lands is equally challenging. Rangeland ecosystems are a collective manifestation of thousands of variables and millions of interactions among those variables. Rangelands don't always "behave" in predictable fashions. Rangelands defy any easy, quick, simplistic encapsulation of their responses to livestock grazing, and they challenge application of any specific, single system, or blueprint, for their management.

There are no simple solutions, and we do a tremendous disservice to our understanding of our environment if we insist on simple explanations. This need for depth in understanding is not new. Over 50 years ago, Lincoln Ellison wrote insightfully about rangelands in an article published in the *Journal of Forestry* (1949, vol. 47: 787-795):

"The man assigned the management of . . .range land faces problems whose final solutions require years of scientific study, but he is expected to deliver immediate answers that are both correct and practical. With the help of a few ecological principles he must be his own scientist, and by observation ascertain what standards he can use

> "Rangelands don't always 'behave' in predictable fashions. Rangelands defy any easy, quick, simplistic encapsulation of their responses to livestock grazing, and they challenge application of any specific, single system, or blueprint, for their management."

for range in ideal condition, on a variety of sites. He must appraise the condition of each site—the character of soil erosion, vegetal cover, and plant composition in relation to the site's potentialities. Finally, he must weigh the evidences of change, to ascertain whether range trend is toward or away from the kind of plant cover and soil stability that is desired."

Today, both genders are involved in land management, but the essence of Ellison's remarks remains relevant. Ellison, and others who worked on and wrote about rangelands during the first half of the 20th century, recognized that these were not simple, easily understood systems. For example, Ellison observed that sites had several potentials, and understanding took years of study. Ellison's remarks also acknowledged that factors other than forage conditions, such as soil stability and species diversity, were important in evaluating the condition of land. Interestingly, later in his article, Ellison used the term "rangeland health" to reflect standards of soil stability and species composition for rangelands. Rangeland health is a term we are returning to today.

## Four Management Objectives

We have made advances since 1949 in our understanding of ecological principles, the mechanisms driving ecological change, and characteristics of ecological sites. In thinking about management of rangelands today, we can build on Ellison's comments of over 50 years ago. We should strive for four objectives in managing livestock grazing on New Mexico's rangelands. 1) We should have some understanding of the ecological processes that characterize specific grazed environments. 2) We should know local conditions that modify those ecological processes within these environments. 3) We should monitor grazed environments in order to evaluate ecological responses to management. 4) We should be able to adjust management actions appropriately in response to monitored observations. Working

towards these objectives can create a knowledge base for grazing management.

Ecosystems are defined as communities of organisms and their environment. In reality, communities and their respective environments can span from microscopic to global scales. Most often though, we probably think of ecosystems in scales we interact with, characterized by distinctive plant assemblages across the landscape. We know a tremendous amount about individual processes characteristic of our ecosystems, but much less about their collective interactions. We know a lot about the effects of drivers (drought and fire, for example), but less about how to drive the system ourselves. We know a tremendous amount about past manifestations of these ecosystems, and much less about future trajectories.

This confession of insufficient knowledge should not be discounted as a typical lament of a scientist. It's understood that we will never have complete knowledge, and that management decisions and public policy regarding rangelands will continue to be made from a limited knowledge base. However, it is important to recognize that we understand some pieces of the ecosystem puzzle, but many pieces need more clarification, and there is no one set way to manage the pieces of all our different environments. What we strive for is sustainability.

## Sustainability

In general, sustainability refers to the maintenance of ecological integrity over time. However, an exact definition of "sustainability" has been elusive. It has been argued that the application of sustainability to rangelands is nonsensical for two reasons. First, rangelands are dynamic and subject to change, defying the notion of long-term stability. Second, ecosystems by definition sustain use or they would cease to exist. Yet, if human use of rangelands is considered, and some economically based use is involved, the concept of sustainable use as a goal has value.

Sustainable use can be defined as an appropriation of production (such as biomass used by grazing livestock) that allows for natural processes to replace appropriated materials. This means that standards of use or consumption are, in some fashion, gauged to the natural limits of an ecosystem. This is what the melding of ecological principles and grazing management is all about today, and is what Ellison was trying to convey in his article in 1949. Thus, at the center of grazing management is the need to be able to evaluate rangeland environments.

## Management Problems

Our primary problems related to management of livestock grazing are those we have continually dealt with throughout the 20th and into the 21st century: 1) coping with variations (spatial and temporal) in forage production, 2) manipulating an animal behavior process (grazing) that is plant-species specific, and 3) managing grazing across landscapes with limited (if any) measurements to monitor or assess impacts. Fortunately, there are management tools, such as conservative stocking and seasonal use, prescribed burning, and herding, that are effective in managing these problems.

Basically, though, what we want to manage for is plant production. This is not to be viewed as

> "...there is a tremendous knowledge base related to factors that influence plant production processes that we can employ in our management."

myopically managing for forage production, but as a much broader objective related to the composition and functioning of ecosystems. There are many processes that we can not effectively manage, but key processes related to plant production, such as germination, seedling establishment, and plant growth are processes we can impact.

Additionally, there is a tremendous knowledge base related to factors that influence plant production processes that we can employ in our management. Plant production processes serve as a means for organizing our knowledge about rangelands and structuring our management. For example, plant productivity is strongly controlled by the availability and distribution of water and nutrients. So, it is not just if and when it rains, but how that moisture moves and is stored across the landscape. Other important processes, such as decomposition and mineralization are affected by moisture distribution. We can base our management actions on how we impact properties of these landscapes that are related to these key processes. It is then important that we base our evaluation of our management, our monitoring actions, on indicators of these important properties.

## Monitoring

Currently, we identify three general elements of these systems for monitoring that directly relate to plant production. These are: 1) the types, proportions, and distributions of plants (biotic integrity), 2) soil erosion rates and soil compaction (site stability), and 3) water flows and infiltration capacity (hydrologic function). These elements are linked to observable features of the system which reflect key processes related to the functioning of the system. No one element, or indicator of an element, can be used to judge rangeland health.

Indicators of biotic integrity include plant community composition and distribution, amount of bare ground, diversity of plant functional groups, plant demographics (such as evidence of mortality or decadence), amount of litter, annual production,

and perennial plant reproductive capability.

Indicators of soil and site stability include presence of pedestal plants, soil surface resistance to erosion, extent of soil loss, and extent of wind scoured areas.

Indicators of hydrologic function include presence of rills and gullies, water flow patterns, and distribution of litter.

These and other indicators can be evaluated qualitatively or, in many cases quantitatively, in objective and repeatable fashions. Basing our evaluations on a suite of indicators related to these processes provides an ecological framework for structuring grazing management as a sustainable activity. This also provides us a means for logically and scientifically interacting with these intricate ecosystems. In this manner, we have advanced our management beyond the setting Ellison described in 1949.

## Melding Ecology and Management

There are three central postulates that describe the ecological character of rangelands: 1) vegetation state and the plant communities within those states are often strongly influenced by just a few species, 2) plant dominance within these states and communities is often long-lived, and 3) there are transitions and thresholds as one vegetative state changes to another. The driving forces of these changes are typically environmental stresses, especially drought or prolonged absence of fire, and these stresses can be amplified by mismanagement, especially overgrazing.

We have two primary management options: 1) we can manipulate vegetation structure in direct and indirect ways, and 2) we can affect plant and animal production by

One additional challenge we face in rangeland management is identifying the spatial scale for management. Rangelands are actually a nested set of spatial scales, from individual plants, to plant communities, to landscapes, and to regional scales. Management actions

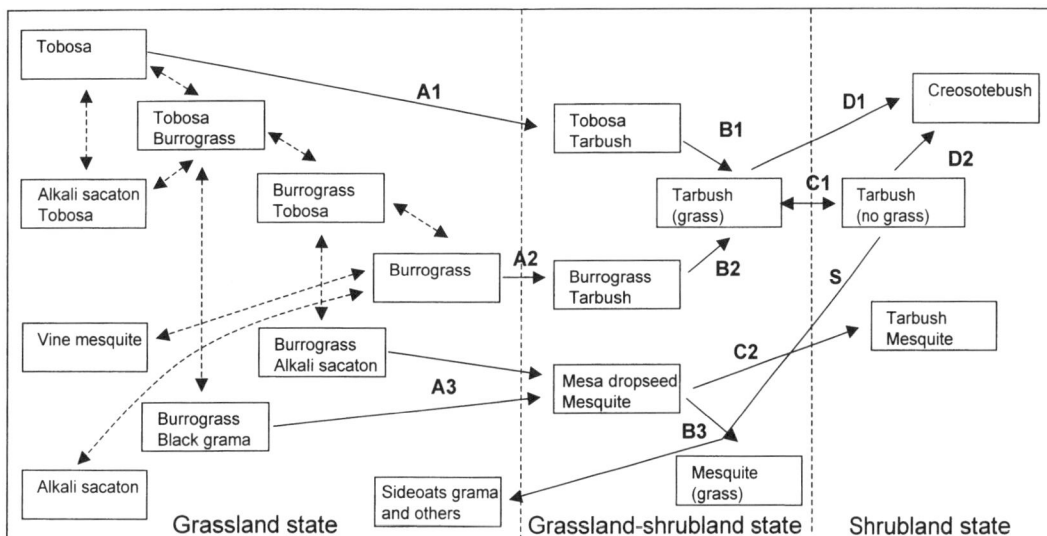

Figure 1. A state and transition model for an ecological site in the Chihuahuan Desert Grassland The solid arrows represent transitions that are known from data collected at the Jornada Experimental Range; the dashed arrows are hypothesized transitions. The vertical, dashed lines are thresholds that divide groups of relatively stable states. (Figure courtesy of Dr. Brandon Bestelmeyer, Jornada Experimental Range).

adjusting our controls over livestock. These options are employed based primarily on the condition of the land. For lands in satisfactory health we manipulate secondary consumers (primarily livestock, but on many ranges this can also include manipulations of wild or feral herbivores). For rangelands at risk, we would direct our attention toward the primary producers (the plants) and affect processes related to plant production. For seriously degraded lands we would gear our attention towards the physical environment (such as methods to rebuild soil). In all cases, our actions require evaluations based on ecological conditions.

need to be structured to spatial scales that can be observed and manipulated in an economical manner. Often, this will be accomplished at relatively small scales. It is unlikely that site-specific information will be available for each managed situation. Management will require application of ecological principles, modifying this application to local conditions, monitoring responses, and adjusting actions based on these observations. This management model represents a melding of our knowledge of range ecology with our knowledge of grazing management practices. It is similar to the process Ellison described, but based on a much-

Figure 2. The various scales at which grazing may be analyzed and understood. (Figure courtesy of Carol Roman and Nathan Sayre.)

a. Individual Plant Scale. An animal grazes the plant at a particular moment in time. Impact is conspicuous but diminishes as the plant recovers over a period of several weeks (during the growing season) or months.

b. Pasture Scale (many plants). Herd of animals grazes over a period of several days to a season, or longer. Impacts develop gradually.

c. Ranch Scale (many pastures). Herd or herds of animals graze on an ongoing basis. Impacts unfold over a period of years.

d. Watershed or Landscape Scale (many ranches). Multiple herds of animals, grazing ongoing, but impacts and conditions vary from ranch to ranch and year to year. Overall impacts may be difficult to evaluate, given the variety of conditions; change may be noticeable only over a period of many years or decades.

improved knowledge base regarding ecological processes and evaluating the health of these rangelands. Today, we label this model "adaptive management." At the center of adaptive management is the same need that Ellison described; we must be educated and practiced observers of our environment.

I'm not sure what someone might write 50 years from now about our current perceptions on rangeland management. I would hope that it would be as complimentary as my assessment of the relevance of Ellison's 1949 remarks. If we base our understanding, our evaluations, and our management on ecological principles, then what we are working toward today should remain relevant. More importantly, working from an ecological basis will ensure that, 50 years from now, we are managing these resources in a sustainable fashion.

# Holy Cow! Biodiversity on Ranches, Developments, and Protected Areas in the "New West"

*by Jeremy D. Maestas, Richard L. Knight, and Wendell C. Gilgert*

Richard Knight is interested in the ecological effects associated with the conversion of the Old West to a New West. A professor of wildlife conservation at Colorado State University, he received his graduate degrees from the University of Washington and the University of Wisconsin. While at Wisconsin, he was an Aldo Leopold Fellow and conducted his research at Aldo Leopold's farm, living in "The Shack." Before becoming an academic, he worked for the Washington Department of Game developing the non-game wildlife program. Presently, he sits on a number of boards including The Society for Conservation Biology, the Colorado Cattlemen's Agricultural Land Trust, and the Natural Resources Law Center. He is an assigning editor for the journal *Conservation Biology*. Recently, he was selected by the Ecological Society of America for the first cohort of Aldo Leopold Leadership Fellows, who focus on leadership in the scientific community, communicating with the media, and interacting with the business and corporate sectors. With almost 100 articles in peer-reviewed journals and 35 book chapters, Rick enjoys sharing his research findings with others. He has co-edited *Wildlife and Recreationists* (1995, Island Press), *A New Century for Natural Resources Management* (1995, Island Press), *Stewardship Across Boundaries* (1998, Island Press), *The Essential Aldo Leopold* (1999, University of Wisconsin Press), *Forest Fragmentation in the Southern Rocky Mountains* (2000, University Press of Colorado), *Ranching West of the 100th Meridian* (2002, Island Press), and *Aldo Leopold and the Ecological Conscience* (2002, Oxford University Press). With his wife Heather, he works with his neighbors in Livermore Valley on stewardship and community-based activities.

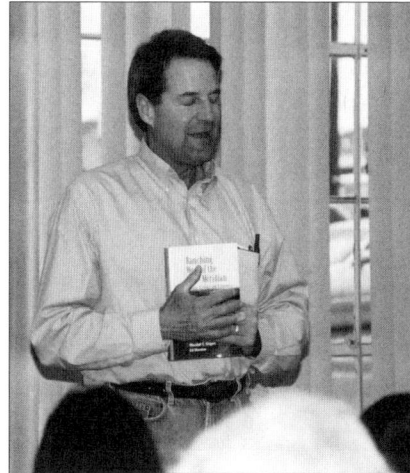

Conservationists have an admirable history of documenting the impacts of human land uses on biodiversity to better inform resource management decisions, but our current knowledge about land-use changes in the Mountain West is less than satisfactory. We work to diminish extractive and commodity-based industries such as water development, logging, mining, and livestock grazing in this region, but we have largely failed to recognize the ecological consequences of our own actions, especially when those actions involve where we choose to live and play. We continue to devote much of our attention to the traditional consumptive land uses that characterized the "Old West," while other threats to biodiversity become more pervasive each year with the emergence of a "New West." For example, urban sprawl and outdoor recreation are the number two and

Subdivision in Wyoming. (Photo courtesy of Dan Dagget.)

number four leading causes, respectively, for the decline of federally listed threatened and endangered species (Czech, Krausman, and Devers 2000).

The character of the New West is being shaped by a flood of immigrants seeking to enjoy the natural amenities and recreational opportunities of a region rich in public lands (Power 1996; Masnick 2001). Importantly, however, the West is only half public lands; the most productive lands in this region

are in private ownership (Scott et al. 2001). This fact becomes critical since the most profound land use change in the New West is the conversion of private lands presently in ranching and farming to rural residential developments (i.e., exurban development) (Knight 2002). Unfortunately, conservationists have given scant attention to studying the ecological implications of this land-use conversion.

Here, we address some of the ecological issues associated with land-use change in the Mountain West.

### Exurbanization of the Mountain West

The Mountain West of the United States is experiencing a human population boom that rivals any in its history. Of the eight states that make up this region (Arizona, Colorado, Idaho, Montana, Nevada, New Mexico, Utah, and Wyoming), five are the fastest growing in the country (Figure 1). Metropolitan areas and their suburbs have accommodated much of this in-migration but rural areas are growing at a faster rate (Heimlich and Anderson 2001). Driven by a mixture of economic and quality-of-life features, people are increasingly drawn to the rural Mountain West (Power 1996).

Jeremy Maestas received his Ph.D. from Colorado State University and is now a wildlife biologist with the Natural Resources Conservation Service (NRCS) in Utah.

Wendell Gilgert is a wildlife biologist with the NRCS Wildlife Habitat Management Institute at Colordato State University in Fort Collins.

Unlike previous booms driven by resource extraction and commodity production, the present period of growth is fueled by the expansion of service, recreation, and information industries and is marked by the conversion in private land use from agriculture to exurban development (Riebsame, Gosnell, and Theobald 1996; Sullins et al. 2002).

As a result, three of the principal land uses in the rural Mountain West today are protection, livestock ranching, and exurban development. Protected areas are lands where residential development is prohibited. Exurban development refers to low-density residential development that occurs beyond incorporated city limits (Nelson and Dueker 1990; Knight 1999). The main human use on protected areas is outdoor recreation and nature protection, on ranches it is livestock production, and on exurban development it is human residence. The amount of land in protection is relatively static with very little being acquired annually. The amount of land in ranching and

exurban development, however, is in flux. Many ranches are being subdivided into exurban developments. For instance, between 1992 and 1997 in Colorado, the rate of agri-

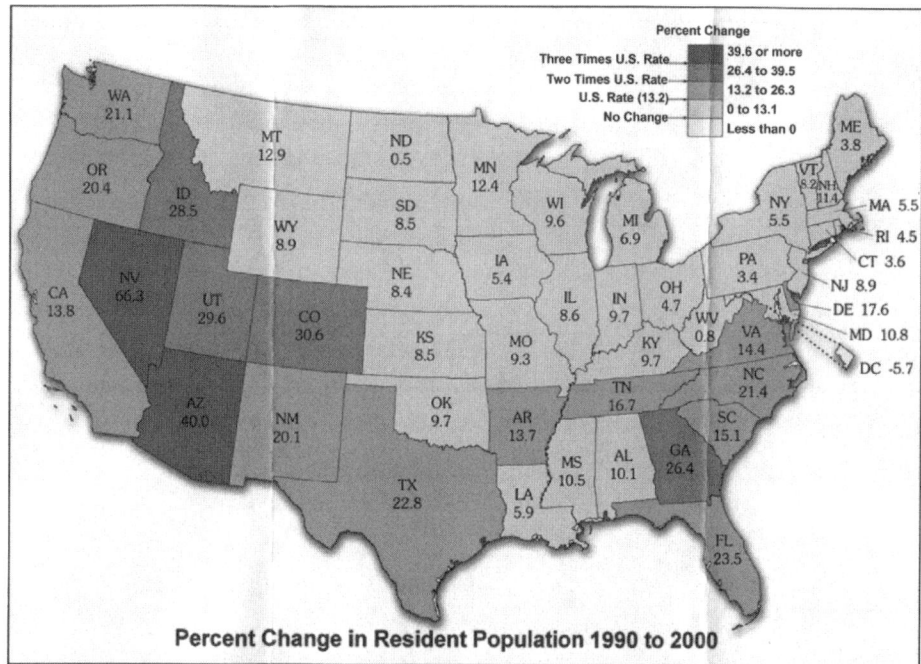

Percent Change in Resident Population 1990 to 2000

Figure 1

cultural land conversion to commercial and residential development was 270,000 acres per year (Oberman, Carlson, and Batchelder 2000).

The extent of land-use change due to population growth in rural areas of the Mountain West is greater than that in urban areas because of the dispersed nature of exurban development (Theobald 2000; Sullins et al. 2002). Instead of focusing growth within incorporated city limits, exurban growth exists as pockets of residential development embedded in a matrix of agricultural and protected lands. Nearly 80% of the land used for houses constructed between 1994 and 1997 in the U.S. was in non-metropolitan areas (Heimlich and Anderson 2001).

in wildlife communities in and around metropolitan areas (e.g., Emlen 1974; Bessinger and Osborne 1982; Mills, Dunning, and Bates 1989; Engels and Sexton 1994; Blair

Table 1. Numbers of wildlife species at different elevations in the San Juan Mountains and adjacent lowlands, Colorado. Note how the lower elevations (private lands) contain more species (Spencer and Romme 1996).

| Feet | 4,600-5,899 | 5,900-7,199 | 7,200-8,499 | 8,500-9,799 | 9,800-11,100 |
|---|---|---|---|---|---|
| Amphibians | 8 | 7 | 5 | 4 | 2 |
| Reptiles | 26 | 17 | 6 | 7 | 1 |
| Mammals | 49 | 53 | 42 | 40 | 37 |

Sites adjacent to public lands are particularly attractive for development (Riebsame, Gosnell, and Theobald 1996; Swanson 2001). Also, exurban developments require more land than urban and suburban developments because each house is situated on a large lot (typically 10-40 acres). Fifty-seven percent of the houses built between 1994 and 1997 were on lots 10 acr es (Heimlich and Anderson 2001). In general, exurban developments increase the influences associated with human residences at two spatial scales: 1) the site scale by dispersed housing, and 2) the landscape scale by the placement of developments in rural areas (Duerksen et al. 2000).

In contrast to urban and suburban development, the ecological consequences of exurban development are not well studied. Many researchers have documented changes

1996; Germaine et al. 1998; Bock, Bock, and Bennett 1999; Crooks and Soulé 1999). Relatively few studies, however, have examined biodiversity associated with exurban developments (Vogel 1989; Harrison 1997, 1998; Odell and Knight 2001), and no studies have compared biodiversity on exurban developments with ranching and protected areas. Although little is known about the conversion of ranchland to exurban development, conservationists have assumed that it results in a simplification of biodiversity, favoring generalist species that thrive in association with humans over those that are more sensitive (Knight and Clark 1998; Knight 2002; Knight et al. 2002).

We know that wildlife habitat is affected directly and indirectly by the conversion of Western ecosystems to exurban development (Knight and Clark 1998). Soil and vegetation are directly disturbed and lost in the construction of houses, roads, fences, and communication lines. Habitat quality is degraded because of the proliferation of non-native plants and the presence of humans, their automobiles, and their pets (Mills, Dunning, and Bates 1989; Knight and Clark 1998; Miller, Knight, and Miller 2001). These changes result in elevated mortality rates, as well as habitat loss and degradation.

## Conservation Response

Concerns over the conversion of the Mountain West's natural heritage from a mixture of generalist and specialist species to one of increasingly human-adapted species have generated a new response to biodiversity protection among nongovernmental conservation organizations (NGOs). The traditional response to protecting biodiversity from anthropogenic degradation has been to purchase land and designate it as a protected area. The emerging response is to work with ranchers to protect biodiversity while keeping the land in private ownership and as a working ranch (Alexander and Propst 2002). Typically, development rights on the ranches are purchased through conservation easements, while ranchers continue to raise livestock. This approach has become increasingly popular, especially among NGOs such as The Nature Conservancy and the Rocky Mountain Elk

Foundation (Weeks 2002). In Colorado, about 86,000 acres of private land have been protected through conservation easements by The Nature Conservancy and 59,000 acres by the Rocky Mountain Elk Foundation (GCOFR 2000). This strategy has increased the number of land trusts that seek to protect private land in agriculture from development. By 2000, over 1,200 land trusts in the United States had protected roughly 2,600,000 acres through conservation easements, 46% of which was farm and ranch-land (LTA 2001).

This emerging response to biodiversity protection, however, has some untested assumptions. It assumes that biodiversity on ranches is no different than that found on protected areas, or at least that biodiversity is better served on ranches than on exurban developments. NGOs are taking this mode of action to protect biodiversity with virtually no scientific evidence to support their approach. They continue with this strategy despite the fact that many environmentalists argue that livestock ranching is perhaps the most detrimental land use in the West (Fleischner 1994; Wuerthner 1994; Donahue 1999). We decided to test these assumptions of the emerging biodiversity protection strategy.

## Study Area and Site Collection

We conducted our study from May through August during 2000 and 2001 in the foothills along

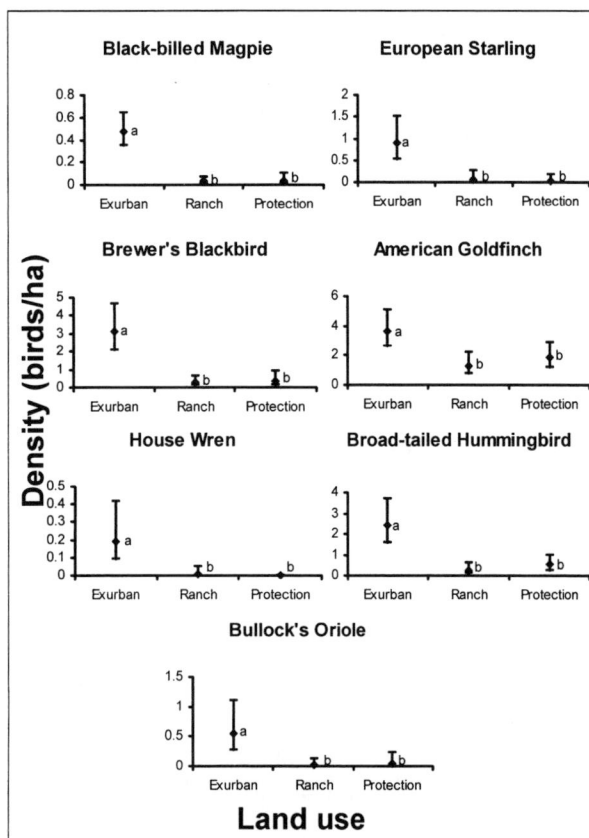

Figure 2

bitterbrush. Common forbs include fringed sage and hairy goldaster. Average annual precipitation ranges from 13-18 inches with 75% of it falling between April and September (U.S. Department of Agriculture 1980).

We restricted our study to sites with similar physical characteristics. We used sites in the same shrubsteppe plant community, with elevations between 5,700-7,200 feet, and similar soil types to reduce natural variability among sites. Study sites had to be greater than 2,500 acres in size to minimize the influence of surrounding land uses. We used 1:24,000 orthophotoquadrangle maps and plat maps from the Larimer County Assessor's Office to determine potential sites. We had 33 out of 35 landowners grant us permission to conduct research on their property.

the Front Range of the Rocky Mountains in northern Larimer County, Colorado. The study area is approximately 25 miles northwest of Fort Collins, the nearest metropolitan area. The land-use matrix of the region is a blend of private ranchland, public protected areas, and exurban developments. The vegetation is a mosaic of shrubsteppe and mixed-grass prairie with some trees occurring at the higher elevations and northern aspects. Dominant grasses include needle-and-thread, blue grama, western wheatgrass, and cheatgrass. Shrubs include mountain mahogany, skunkbrush sumac, and

## Study Design and Data Collection

We compared songbird, mammalian carnivore, and plant communities across three land uses: 1) public protected areas (Colorado Division of Wildlife's State Wildlife Areas) whose principal use was outdoor recreation and wildlife protection (no grazing, logging, mining, or water development), 2) private-land livestock ranches with cattle, and 3) exurban developments with one house per 35-50 acres. We randomly selected 93 points across the three land uses to survey songbirds and mammalian carnivores, and 69 points to sample the plant community. At each randomly selected point, we sampled communities using point counts for songbirds, scent stations for mammalian carnivores, and Daubenmire quadrats for plants.

## Findings

Biodiversity differed across the three land-use categories. Wildlife species occurrence and densities were more similar between ranches and protected areas than on exurban developments. Plant communities on ranches, however, differed from those on protected areas and exurban developments.

We observed a suite of species in the songbird and mammalian carnivore communities that benefit from factors that accompany elevated human densities found in exurban developments. We also found species of songbirds and carnivores that occurred in elevated densities on ranches and protected areas when compared to exurban developments. For the plant communities, native species were more prevalent and non-native species were less prevalent on ranches than on either protected areas or exurban developments. Many of the species that thrive in exurban developments also fare well in suburban and urban settings.

Songbirds occurred in three categories that separated out based on densities and land use. Generalist or human-adapted species reached their greatest densities in exurban developments when compared to ranches and protected areas (Figure

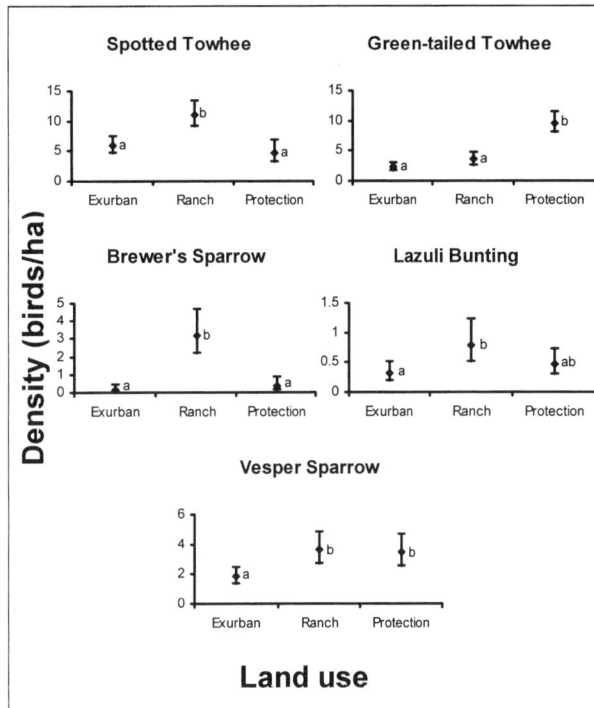

**Figure 3**

2). Species with more narrow ecological niches attained their greatest densities on land devoted to ranching, protection, or both of those land uses when compared to exurban developments (Figure 3). Some songbird species, such as the brown-headed cowbird and rock wren, showed no statistically significant differences in densities across the three land uses.

We did not have large enough sample sizes to generate reliable density estimates for many of the species detected, but it is worth noting some compositional differences observed in these less abundant species. We observed the house finch, common raven, Say's phoebe, and red-winged blackbird only on exurban developments. The dusky flycatcher, savannah sparrow, and lark bunting were seen only on ranches and protected areas.

Few mammalian carnivores were detected over the course of our study. Domestic dogs and house cats were detected almost exclusively on exurban developments, whereas coyotes were seldom found at our scent stations on exurban developments (Figure 4). Bobcats showed no statistical difference at scent

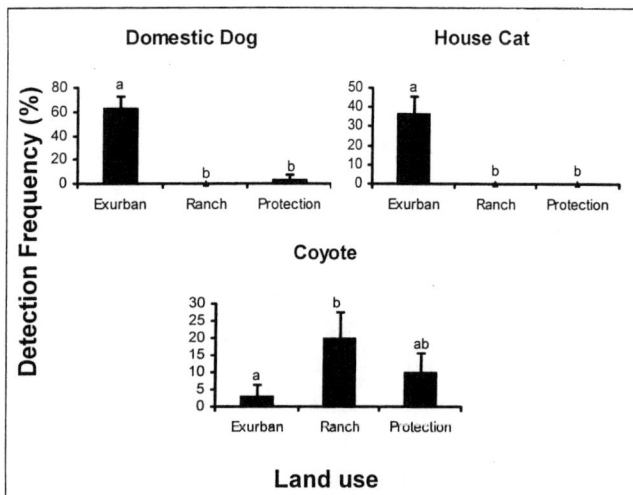

Figure 4.

stations across the three land uses.

The number of species (i.e., species richness) and plant cover differed across the land uses. We recorded the most non-native species on exurban developments (Figure 5). Non-native species richness and cover per point were highest on the exurban developments and protected areas when compared to ranches. More species of native plants were found on ranches than the other two land uses, but the cover of native

plant species did not differ statistically across land uses. The dominant non-native plant, cheatgrass, was more prevalent in terms of cover on the protected areas and exurban developments than on ranches.

**Conservation Implications**

Our results support the emerging strategy for biodiversity protection being implemented by environmental NGOs. Ranches in our study supported a more desirable biodiversity than exurban developments. This is evident for three reasons. First, ranches were virtually the same as protected areas in terms of human-adapted wildlife species. Second, ranches had enhanced populations of native wildlife species of conservation concern compared to exurban developments. Third, plant communities on ranches had more native species, fewer non-native species, and less non-native plant cover than exurban developments.

A more ambiguous relationship exists between ranches and protected areas. The assumption that these two land uses support similar biodiversity is only partially borne out by our observations. Ranches and protected areas supported similarly low populations of human-adapted wildlife species but produced variable populations of other species. Also, protected areas had a higher prevalence of non-native plant species and fewer native plant species than ranches.

A generalization from our study is that there is an increase in human-adapted wildlife and non-native plant species with exurban development. Interactions among native, non-native, and human-adapted species could result in the simplification of the Mountain West's natural heritage, favoring species whose evolutionary life histories allow them to exist with humans. This change has negative implications for the maintenance of biodiversity at both the site and landscape scales, and its consequences are increased with increasing development (Knight 2002).

**Songbirds.** Elevated populations of human-adapted songbirds may be occurring to the detriment of other species (Marzluff, Gehlbach, and Manuwal 1998). For instance, nest predators such as the black-billed magpie may lower the reproductive success of other birds in an area. The blue jay, a similar nest predator, has been shown to increase with urbanization and play an important role in the decline of an endangered bird, the golden-cheeked warbler (Engels and Sexton 1994). The non-native European starling is an aggressive competitor with native birds for nesting cavities. In one area in Nevada, starlings were successful at excluding native birds from nest sites for five years (Weitzel 1988). Eric Odell and Richard Knight (2001) studied songbirds on exurban developments and undeveloped areas, and found exurban developments supported the greatest densities of black-billed magpies and European starlings and the lowest densities of

other songbirds, which may be attributed to interactions between these species.

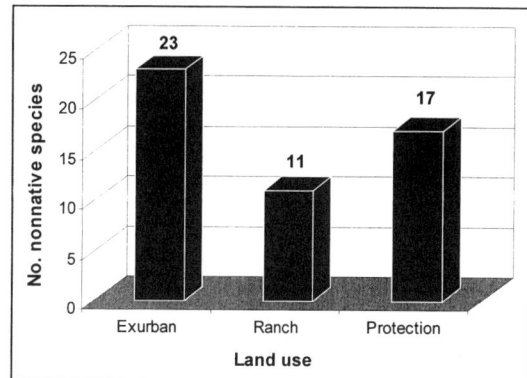

Figure 5

**Pets.** House cats and domestic dogs are subsidized predators that have been shown to extend the realm of human influence and have substantial impacts on wildlife populations (Churcher and Lawton 1987; Miller, Knight, and Miller 2001). These free-ranging pets can occur at elevated densities, as seen in our study, because they are supplementally fed and are not dependent on densities of native prey species. House cats have been implicated in the decline and extinction of scrub-breeding songbirds in two studies in California (Hawkins 1998; Crooks and Soulé 1999). Furthermore, Kevin Crooks and Michael Soulé (1999) found that songbirds persisted in patches with coyotes because these native predators depressed house cat numbers. Coyotes were detected less frequently in exurban developments than in the other land uses in our study, which could result in unusually high songbird mortality from domestic cats. Domestic dogs are known to harass and kill wildlife, but their impacts are less well studied. Research has shown that they can extend the zone of human influence and contribute to the annual mortality of some species (Miller, Knight, and Miller 2001; Ballard et al. 1999). Domestic dogs and house cats have been

processes and degrading the quality of wildlife habitat (Masters and Sheley 2001). For instance, cheatgrass proliferation in the Mountain West has altered historic fire

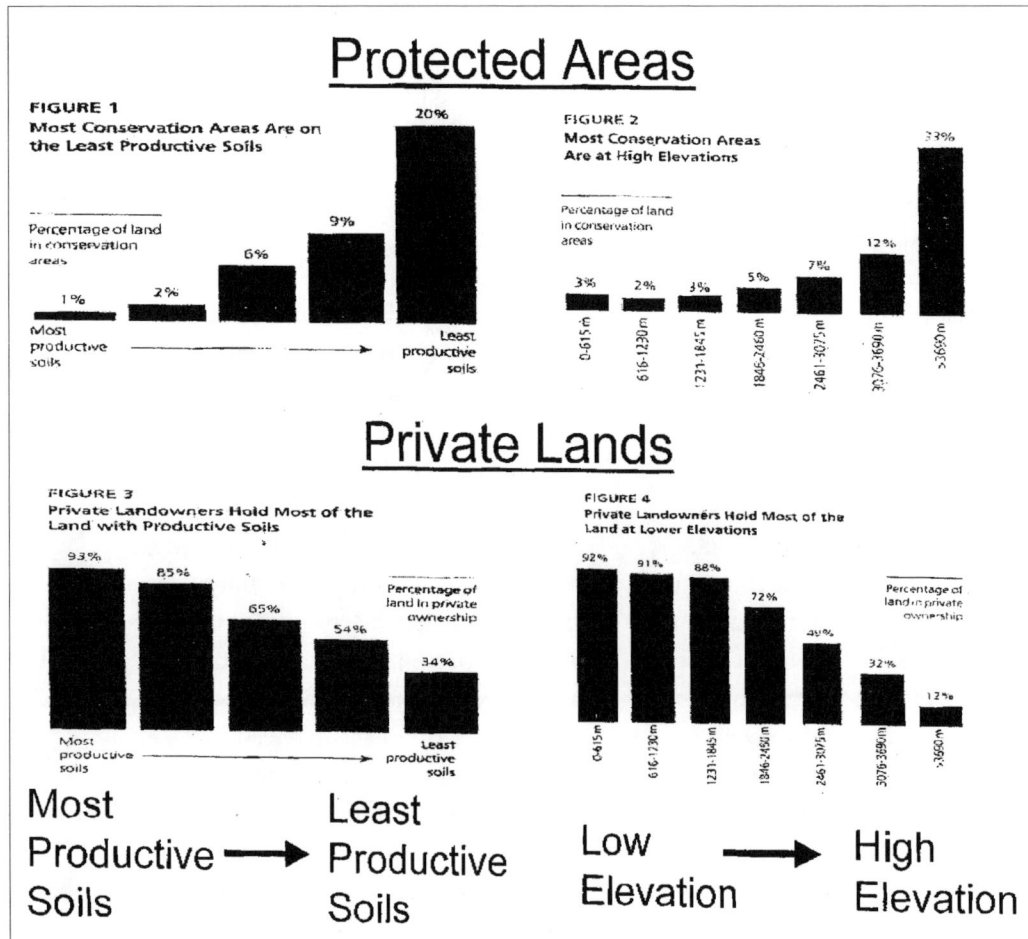

Figure 6. The distribution of public lands and lands in private ownership, by soil and elevation. Note that private lands occur at the lowest elevations and on the most productive soils.

documented to be more prevalent in exurban developments, especially near houses, possibly at the expense of other native predators which were less abundant in exurban developments than undeveloped areas (Odell and Knight 2001).

Non-Native Species. Non-native plants can change community dynamics by disrupting ecosystem

regimes, favoring non-native, annual grasslands over native, perennial species. This invasive plant has displaced native plants and altered the occurrence of shrub-obligate songbirds that utilize these ecosystems (Rotenberry 1998). In our study, eight of 23 non-native plant species were found only in exurban developments. Two of these species, spotted knapweed and leafy spurge, are noxious weeds that have been shown to lower the value of rangeland ecosystems for ungulates such as deer and elk (Trammell and Butler 1995; Thompson 1996).

The results of altered biotic communities in exurban developments could be influential at two spatial scales (Duerksen et al. 2000). At the site scale, potential interactions among wildlife species suggest that exurban developments may be functioning as *ecological traps:* areas where species assess the land to be suitable habitat but then suffer reduced survival and reproduction when they live there (Pulliam 1996; Donovan and Thompson 2001). Also at this level, non-native plants displace native plants, thereby altering interspecific dynamics and reducing habitat quality for wildlife that do best in native plant communities. At the landscape scale, exurban developments could be serving as sources that produce an excess of human-adapted wildlife species and non-native plants. Because exurban developments are embedded in rural areas, often adjacent to public lands, they may be providing individuals and propagules that spill over into surrounding lands. Therefore, the effects of exurban development are not just within its boundaries but well onto other areas (Buechner and Sauvajot 1996; Theobald, Miller, and Hobbs 1997; Knight and Clark 1998).

If exurban developments are sources of undesirable species, then the emerging strategy to protect biodiversity by working with ranchers is correct. Ranchers and farmers own much of the land being converted to exurban development in the Mountain West (Theobald 2000). Our study found that biodiversity was at least as well served on ranches

> "Our study found that biodiversity was at least as well served on ranches as it was on protected areas."

as it was on protected areas. More support for the new conservation strategy is provided by a recent study that pointed out that most of our protected areas lie on the least productive soils and at the highest elevations, whereas most private lands occur on the most productive, low elevation sites (Figure 6) (Scott et al. 2001). Our results combined with this information suggest that we will not be able to sustain native biodiversity in the Mountain West by relying merely on protected areas. Future conservation efforts to protect this region's natural heritage will require closer attention being paid to the role of private lands (Knight 1999).

## Considerations for Land-Use Decisionmakers

Inferences from our study should be viewed as speculative, but if further studies support our findings, land-use planners need to be aware of the ecological effects of exurban developments across the Mountain West. The Ecological Society of America recently published a report that provided ecological principles and guidelines for land-use decisions (Dale et al. 2000). Christopher Duerksen and others (2000) have written a useful handbook that gives suggestions for reducing human impacts associated with housing developments. Decisionmakers concerned about the sustainability of land uses and the maintenance of biodiversity should consult these documents and others, and encourage more informed conversations about the implications of land-use decisions. We suggest three additional points, derived from an ecological perspective, to consider when making land-use decisions in the rural Mountain West:

*(1) Development location is ecologically relevant.* Low-elevation lands support a disproportionate amount of biodiversity and can be the most ecologically sensitive (Romme 1997). Additionally, the effects of development extend beyond its boundaries and can be expected to influence surrounding lands. Strategic placement of exurban developments within a rural landscape is critical (Knight and Clark 1998).

*(2) Low-density residential developments influence biotic communities.* Even at densities of one house per 35-50 acres, the effects of human

residences are seen. It cannot be assumed that, because most of the land within exurban developments remains undeveloped, it is suitable for all species that would occur there if houses were not present. Exurban development patterns spread the influence associated with human developments further across the landscape than more concentrated development densities, such as urban and suburban. Laws that exclude certain development densities from the county review process should be reevaluated. For example, Colorado law allows subdivisions of 1 house per 35 acres or greater to avoid county review, therefore encouraging this density of development (Riebsame, Gosnell, and Theobald 1996; Romme 1997). Cluster developments are an alternative settlement pattern that involves concentrating houses and leaving the remainder of the purchased land undeveloped (Theobald, Miller, and Hobbs 1997; Odell and Knight 2001). However, little is known about the site- and landscape-scale effects of cluster development, so caution should be used in promoting this approach.

*(3) Ranches are important in biodiversity protection.* Because private lands are often the most productive, lowest elevation sites, they play a disproportionate role in maintaining biodiversity that is not found on protected areas, which are mostly on the least productive, high elevation sites (Scott and others 2001). Ranches in our study area

were as good or better as comparable protected areas at conserving biodiversity. Conversion of ranch-land to exurban development should be monitored because it will likely result in a simplification of our natural heritage and an ever increasing number of species with declining populations.

## References

Alexander, B., and L. Propst. 2002. Saving the Family Ranch: New Directions. In *Ranching West of the 100th Meridian*, edited by R. L. Knight, W. C. Gilgert, and E. Marston, 203–217. Washington, D.C.: Island Press.

Ballard, W. B., H. A. Whitlaw, S. J. Young, R. A. Jenkins, and G. J. Forbes. 1999. Predation and Survival of White-Tailed Deer Fawns in Northcentral New Brunswick. *Journal of Wildlife Management* 63 (2): 574–579.

Beissinger, S. R. and D. R. Osborne. 1982. Effects of Urbanization on Avian Community Organization. *Condor* 84: 75–83.

Blair, R. B. 1996. Land Use and Avian Species Diversity along an Urban Gradient. *Ecological Applications* 6 (2): 506–519.

Bock, C. E., J. H. Bock, and B. C. Bennett. 1999. Songbird Abundance in Grasslands at a Suburban Interface on the Colorado High Plains. *Studies in Avian Biology* 19: 131–136.

Buechner, M., and R. Sauvajot. 1996. Conservation and Zones of Human Activity: The Spread of Human Disturbance across a Protected Landscape. In *Biodiversity in Managed Landscapes*, edited by R. C. Szaro and D. W. Johnston, 605–629. New York: Oxford University Press.

Churcher, P. B. and J. H. Lawton. 1987. Predation by Domestic Cats in an English Village. *Journal of Zoology, London* 212: 439–455.

Crooks, K. R., and M. E. Soulé. 1999. Mesopredator Release and Avifaunal Extinctions in a Fragmented System. *Nature* 400: 563–566.

Czech, B., P. R. Krausman, and P. K. Devers. 2000. Economic Associations Among Causes of Species Endangerment in the United States. *BioScience* 50 (7): 593–601.

Dale, V. H., S. Brown, R. A. Haeuber, N. T. Hobbs, N. Huntly, R. J. Naiman, W. E. Riebsame, M. G. Turner, and T. J. Valone. 2000. Ecological Principles and Guidelines for Managing the Use of Land. *Ecological Applications* 10 (3) 639–670.

Donahue, D. L. 1999. *The Western Range Revisited: Removing Livestock from Public Lands to Conserve Native Biodiversity.* Norman, OK: University of Oklahoma Press.

Donovan, T. M., and F. R. Thompson, III. 2001. Modeling the Ecological Trap Hypothesis: A Habitat and Demographic Analysis for Migrant Songbirds. *Ecological Applications* 11: 871–882.

Duerksen, C. J., N. T. Hobbs, D. L. Elliot, E. Johnson, and J. R. Miller. 2000. Managing Development for People and Wildlife: A Handbook for Habitat Protection by Local Governments. [http://ndis.nrel.colostate.edu/escop/handbook/intro.html].

Emlen, J. T. 1974. An Urban Bird Community in Tuscson, Arizona: Derivation, Structure, Regulation. *Condor* 76: 184–197.

Engels, T. M. and C. W. Sexton. 1994. Negative Correlation of Blue Jays and Golden-Cheeked Warblers near an Urbanizing Area. *Conservation Biology* 8

(1): 286–290.

Fleischner, T. L. 1994. Ecological Costs of Livestock Grazing in Western North America. *Conservation Biology* 8 (3): 629–644.

Germaine, S. S., S. S. Rosenstock, R. E. Schweinsburg, and W. S. Richardson. 1998. Relationships among Breeding Birds, Habitat, and Residential Development in Greater Tucson, Arizona. *Ecological Applications* 8 (3): 680–691.

GCOFR [Governor's Commission on Saving Open Spaces, Farms, and Ranches]. 2000. Natural Landscapes: Colorado's Legacy to its Children. [www.state.co.us/ issuesopen_space8.pdf].

Harrison, R. L. 1997. A Comparison of Gray Fox Ecology between Residential and Undeveloped Rural Landscapes. *Journal of Wildlife Management* 61 (1): 112–122.

———. 1998. Bobcats in Residential Areas: Distribution and Homeowner Attitudes. *Southwestern Naturalist* 43 (4): 469–475.

Hawkins, C. C. 1998. Impact of a Subsidized Exotic Predator on Native Biota: Effect of House Cats (*Felis catus*) on California Birds and Rodents. Ph.D. diss., Texas A & M University, College Station.

Heimlich, R. E., and W. D. Anderson. 2001. Development at the Urban Fringe and Beyond: Impacts on Agriculture and Rural Land. ERS Agricultural Economic Report No. 803. Washington, D. C.: GPO.

Knight, R. L. 2002. The Ecology of Ranching. In *Ranching West the 100ᵗʰ Meridian*, edited by R. L. Knight, W. C. Gilgert, and E. Marston, 123–144. Washington, D.C.: Island Press.

———. 1999. Private Lands: The Neglected Geography. *Conservation Biology* 13 (2): 223–224.

Knight, R. L., and T. W. Clark. 1998. Boundaries Between Public and Private Lands: Defining Obstacles, Finding Solutions. In *Stewardship across Boundaries*, edited by R. L. Knight and P. B. Landres, 175–191. Washington, D.C.: Island Press.

Knight, R. L., J. Mitchell, E. Odell, and J. Maestas. 2002. Subdividing the West. In *Principles of Conservation Biology*, edited by M. Groom, G. K. Meffe and C. R. Carroll, xxx–xxx. 3d ed. Sunderland, MA: Sinauer Associates.

Linhart, S. B. and F. F. Knowlton. 1975. Determining the Relative Abundance of Coyotes by Scent Station Lines. *Wildlife Society Bulletin* 3 (3): 119–124.

LTA [Land Trust Alliance]. 2001. Summary Data from the National Land Trust Census. [www.lta.org/ newsroom/census_summary_data.htm].

Marzluff, J. M., and F. R. Gehlbach, and D. A. Manuwal. 1998. Urban Environments: Influences on Avifauna and Challenges for the Avian Conservationist. In *Avian Conservation: Research and Management*, edited by J. M. Marzluff and R. Sallabanks, 283–299. Washington, D.C.: Island Press.

Masnick, G. 2001. America's Shifting Population: Understanding Migration Patterns in the West. *Changing Landscapes* 2: 8–15.

Masters, R. A., and R. L. Sheley. 2001. Principles and Practices for Managing Rangeland Invasive Plants. *Journal of Range Management* 54 (5): 502–517.

Miller, S. G., R. L. Knight, and C. K. Miller. 2001. Wildlife Responses to Pedestrians and Dogs. *Wildlife Society Bulletin* 29 (1): 124–132.

Mills, S. G., J. B. Dunning, Jr., and J. M. Bates. 1989. Effects of Urbanization on Breeding Bird Community Structure in Southwestern Desert Habitats. *Condor* 91: 416–428.

Nelson, A. C., and K. J. Dueker. 1990. The Exurbanization of America and its Planning Policy Implications. *Journal of Planning and Education Research* 9 (2): 91–100.

Oberman, B., D. Carlson, and J. Batchelder, eds. 2000. Tracking Agricultural Land Conversion in Colorado. Colorado Department of Agriculture. [www.ag.state.co.us/resource/AgricluturalLandConversion.html]

Odell, E. A., and R. L. Knight. 2001. Songbird and Medium-Sized Mammal Communities associated with Exurban Development in Pitkin County, Colorado. *Conservation Biology* 15 (4): 1143–1150.

Power, T. M. 1996. *Lost Landscapes and Failed Economies.* Washington, D.C.: Island Press.

Pulliam, H. R. 1996. Sources and Sinks: Empirical Evidence and Population Consequences. In *Population Dynamics in Ecological Space and Time*, edited by O. E. Rhodes, Jr., R. K. Chesser, and M. H. Smith, 45–69. Chicago, IL: University of Chicago Press.

Riebsame, W. E., H. Gosnell, and D. M. Theobald. 1996. Land Use and Landscape Change in the Colorado Mountains I: Theory, Scale, and Pattern. *Mountain Research and Development* 16 (4): 395–405.

Romme, W. H. 1997. Creating Pseudo-Rural Landscapes in the Mountain West. In *Placing Nature: Culture and Landscape Ecology*, edited by J. I. Nassauer, 140–161. Covelo, CA: Island Press.

Rotenberry, J. T. 1998. Avian Conservation Research Needs in Western Shrublands: Exotic Invaders and the Alteration of Ecosystem Processes. In *Avian Conservation: Research and Management*, edited by J. M. Marzluff and R. Sallabanks, 261–272. Washington, D.C.: Island Press.

SAS Institute, Inc. 1999. *SAS/STAT® User's Guide, Version 8.0.* Cary, NC: SAS Institute.

Scott, J. M., F. W. Davis, R. G. McGhie, R. G. Wright, C. Groves, and J. Estes. 2001. Nature Reserves: Do They Capture the Full Range of America's Biological Diversity? *Ecological Applications* 11 (4): 999–1007.

Sullins, M. J., D. T. Theobald, J. R. Jones, and L. M. Burgess. 2002. Lay of the Land: Ranch Land and Ranching. In *Ranching West of the 100ᵗʰ Meridian*, edited by R. L. Knight, W. C. Gilgert, and E. Marston, 25–31. Washington, D.C.: Island Press.

Swanson, L. 2001. The West's Forest Lands: Magnets for New Migrants and Part-Time Residents. *Changing Landscape* 2: 16–25.

Theobald, D. M. 2000. Fragmentation by Inholdings and Exurban Development. In *Forest Fragmentation in the Southern Rocky Mountains*, edited by R. L. Knight, F. H. Smith, S. W. Buskirk, W. H. Romme, and W. L. Baker, 155–174. Boulder, CO: University Press of Colorado.

Theobald, D. M., J. R. Miller, and N. T. Hobbs. 1997. Estimating the Cumulative Effects of Development on Wildlife Habitat. *Landscape and Urban Planning* 39: 25–36.

Thomas, L., J. L. Laake, J. F. Derry, S. T. Buckland, D. L. Borchers, D. R. Anderson, K. P. Burnham, S. Strindberg, S. L. Hedley, M. L. Burt, F. Marques, J. H. Pollard, and R. M.

Fewster. 1998. University of St. Andrews, UK: Distance 3.5. Research Unit for Wildlife Population Assessment.

Thompson, M. J. 1996. Winter Foraging Response of Elk to Spotted Knapweed Removal. *Northwest Science* 70: 10–19.

Trammell, M. A., and J. L. Bulter. 1995. Effects of Exotic Plants on Native Ungulate Use of Habitat. *Journal of Wildlife Management* 59 (4): 808–816.

U.S. Department of Agriculture. Soil Conservation Service and Forest Service. 1980. *Soil Survey of Larimer County, Colorado.* Washington, D.C.: GPO 239–812/48.

Vogel, W. O. 1989. Response of Deer to Density and Distribution of Housing in Montana. *Wildlife Society Bulletin* 17 (4): 406–413.

Weeks, W. W. 2002. Cloudy Sky over The Range: Whose Home and Why it Matters. In *Ranching West of the 100th Meridian*, edited by R. L. Knight, W. C. Gilgert, and E. Marston, 219–231. Washington, D.C.: Island Press.

Weitzel, N. H. 1988. Nest-Site Competition between the European Starling and Native Breeding Birds in Northwestern Nevada. *The Condor* 90: 515–517.

Wuerthner, G. 1994. Subdivisions versus Agriculture. *Conservation Biology* 8 (3): 905–908.

# Where Have All the Grasslands Gone?
*by Craig Allen*

Craig Allen is a research ecologist with the U.S. Geological Survey, and is the station leader of the Jemez Mountains Field Station based at Bandelier National Monument. He has worked as a place-based ecologist with the Department of Interior in the Jemez Mountains since 1986. Craig conducts research on the ecology and environmental history of Southwestern landscapes, and provides technical support in the areas of conservation biology and ecological restoration to land management agencies in the region. Craig has been working to coordinate initial natural resource inventory and monitoring efforts in support of adaptive management at the Valles Caldera National Preserve. Craig lives in Los Alamos with his wife Sharon and their three children.

Passing through the majestic landscapes of northern New Mexico today one finds valleys thick with sagebrush, dense woodlands of piñon and juniper amidst eroding foothills, crowded forests of ponderosa pine and fir cloaking plateaus and mountain slopes, and a variety of grasslands and meadows densely fringed with young trees. Most people think of these wildlands as "natural," pretty much the ways things have always been. Yet old-timers and even older documents tell of pine forests and woodlands with grassy understories open enough to drive a wagon through, while ecologists and environmental historians compile ever-increasing evidence of major vegetation changes over the past century. A repeated theme of these ecological histories is the decline in herbaceous vegetation (grasses and non-woody flowering plants) while forests thicken and brush invades. The details of species and timing vary a bit between studies, but everywhere woody plants (trees and shrubs) are increasingly dominant. Why has this been happening?

## The Role of Fire

The main reason for this increase in woody plants in northern New Mexico is human-caused changes in the role of fire in our landscapes. Vegetation patterns are determined by many factors, with climate, topography, and soils often considered paramount. It is less well recognized that disturbances like fires and floods may be equally influential. Particularly here in the Southwest, fire is a key process that determines the ecological structure and function of most ecosystems. In

Apache Canyon, 1945.

general, fire favors grassy vegetation over woody plants. Trees and shrubs can be killed or severely damaged by fire, while perennial grasses not only survive and quickly recover (the same way they regrow from basal growth points after being grazed), their growth may even be enhanced by fire. A variety of scientific studies show that fires have been frequent and widespread in the lands of Rio Arriba since before the Oñate entrada, shaping the vegetation in ways that favored herbaceous lifeforms. About 100 years ago, the occurrence of fire greatly diminished across this region, resulting in major vegetation changes that included declines in grassy vegetation and

increases in woody plants—a trend that continues today.

How do scientists learn about these changes? Researchers have been using a variety of methods to study the history of landscape change in the Southwest, ranging from ecological studies of soil and vegetation to historic records and photographs. Additional details on some of these methods and a variety of results for New Mexico are graphically displayed and referenced at a "Land Use History of North America" website, assembled by Julio Betancourt, Tom Swetnam, and myself, (http://biology.usgs.gov/luhna/southwest/southwest.html).

## Tree and Shrub Invasion of Open Grasslands

Consider the decline of montane grasslands in the Jemez Mountains, which are found on the upper, south-facing slopes of nearly all of the larger summits and ridge crests. These are the most productive grasslands in New Mexico, and their deep, prairie-type soils indicate that grasslands have persisted for thousands of years on these sites. Yet today a tidal wave of young ponderosa pine, Douglas fir, and aspen are observed to be invading these grasslands. By coring and dating hundreds of trees, I found that the tree invasion began in the 1920s. Vegetation mapping from a time sequence of aerial photographs confirms the timing of the tree invasion and reveals the extensiveness of the tree encroachment. Between 1935 and 1981, tree invasion reduced the area of open montane grasslands by 55% across the 250,000 acre mapped area that covers the southeastern Jemez Mountains. Several small montane grasslands present in 1935 have disappeared, while the larger grasslands have become fragmented.

Similar tree and shrub invasions are also observed in many other open vegetation types throughout northern New Mexico, including blue spruce encroachment on moist meadows, Engelmann spruce invasion of subalpine parks in the Pecos Wilderness, and the spread of juniper and sagebrush and snakeweed into valley grasslands. These patterns of woody invasion into formerly grassy environments are tied to changes in land use history, primarily livestock grazing and fire suppression, that are described below.

Apache Canyon, 1984, showing piñon-juniper encroachment. (Photos courtesy of the New Mexico Museum of Natural History.)

## Tales that Trees Tell: Fires in the Forests

One particularly useful approach to uncover local ecological histories has been to use dendrochronological (tree-ring) methods to reconstruct patterns of fire occurrence and forest change over the last several hundred years, primarily in the Jemez Mountains but also in the Sangre de Cristos. Old trees can tell many stories if one knows how to decipher the information contained in their wood. This tree-ring work is being accomplished through a cooperative effort involving the U.S. Geological Survey's Jemez Mountains Field Station (located at Bandelier National Monument), Professor Tom Swetnam's group at the Laboratory of

Tree-Ring Research (University of Arizona), and the Santa Fe and Carson National Forests. Since 1988 we have determined over 4,000 prehistoric fire dates from fire scars

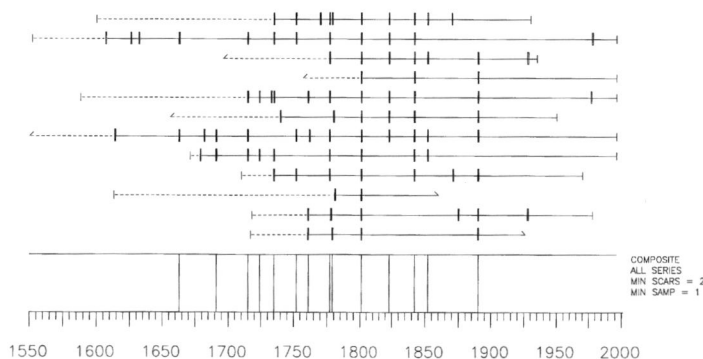

Figure 1. Fire scar chronology for El Valle (near Las Trampas). Horizontal lines represent the life spans of individual trees, while fire scar events are shown by short vertical bars. The longer vertical lines at the bottom of each chronology indicate the dates of fire events in which at least two sampled trees recorded a fire.

on more than 550 sampled trees, snags, logs, and stumps at 30 sites in the Jemez Mountains. In the Sangre de Cristos, we have about 170 prehistoric fire dates from over 50 sampled trees at four sites. Elevations of sampled sites ranged between about 6,500 and 11,000 feet; vegetation varied correspondingly from piñon-juniper woodlands up through ponderosa pine to mixed conifer and spruce forests. Each scar is dated to its precise year of formation, and in most cases, even the season in which the fire occurred was determined. Fire dates extend back to 1422 AD in the Jemez Mountains and to 1230 AD in the Sangre de Cristos.

The fire scar histories show that fire was frequent and widespread at most sites prior to the 1890s. For example, fire scar samples from El Valle (near Las Trampas) record 35 different fire years between 1607 and 1890 AD (Figure 1), while Monument Canyon in the Jemez Moun-

tains records 47 fires from 1591 to 1892 AD (Figure 2). It must be emphasized that these were largely surface fires burning with low-intensity in primarily grassy fuels.

These low-intensity fires thinned the forest by killing some of the younger trees, while most mature trees survived unscathed, protected by their thick bark. Trees that were damaged but not killed by a fire often developed an open wound which was subject to repeated scarring by subsequent fires—some Jemez trees recorded over 30 fires without being killed. The frequent fires stimulated the growth of herbaceous plants in the open forests, prevented the buildup of thick layers of needles and excessive amounts of dead wood, and promoted the rapid cycling of nutrients for plant growth.

Widespread fires occurred about every 5-20 years wherever ponderosa pine grew, with somewhat lower frequencies on the order of 15-40 years in the bracketing piñon-juniper woodlands below and mixed conifer forests above. Although some small, patchy fires certainly occurred, note how in some years almost every tree recorded a fire scar, indicating widespread fire occurrence (Figures 1 and 2). Indeed, in many years, climate-synchronized fires burned throughout whole mountain ranges, and about four times per century most of the mountain ranges across the entire Southwest burned in the same year. With few barriers and without human efforts to contain them, pre-1900 fires may have burned for months in some of these dry years. The position of the fire scars within the annual growth rings indicates that the vast majority of prehistoric fires were occurring in the dry spring period (April-June) before the onset of the summer rains, which is still when most fire activity occurs. Given our dry spring climate and frequent thunderstorms, lightning is believed to have caused the vast majority of these fires. This view is supported by the records of about 4,000 lightning-caused fires documented by firefighters in the Jemez Mountains from 1909-1996, and by the over 160,000 lightning strikes recorded over the Jemez country by a lightning detection system between 1985 and 1994.

Just like nowadays, the most active fire years occurred after dry winters. The most widespread fire activity in ponderosa pine forests typically occurred in dry periods a year or two after wet years in which herbaceous fuels would have built up (another clue about how widespread and important grassy understories were in these open forests).

Note that crown fires were a natural occurrence in some of the higher elevation, wetter, forest types (such as spruce-fir and some mixed conifer forests) where surface fires were less frequent and fuel loads

greater. Places where aspen stands grow today often reflect a history of crown fire. Crown fires took place in particularly dry years, like the spring of 1880 when the spruce forests on Santa Fe Baldy burned.

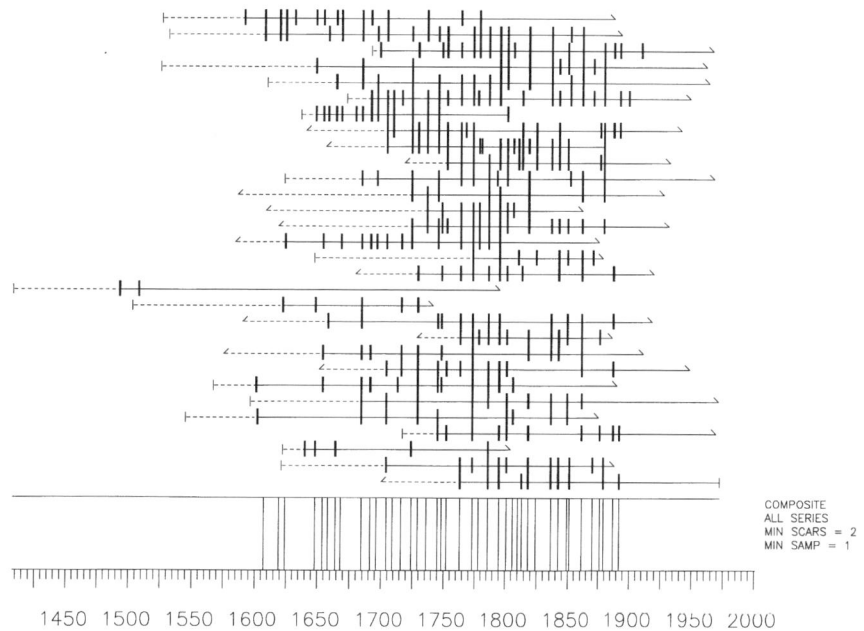

Figure 2. Fire scar chronologies for Monument Canyon Research Natural Area, in the Jemez Mountains. Horizontal lines represent the life spans of individual trees, while fire scar events are shown by short vertical bars. The longer vertical lines at the bottom of each chronology indicate the dates of fire events in which at least two sampled trees recorded a fire.

## What Happened When Surface Fires Ceased?

The widespread surface fires ceased throughout northern New Mexico in the late 1800s (Figures 1 and 2). Railroads reached the lands of Rio Arriba in the 1880s, connecting this region to outside markets and capital, which resulted in a massive boom in livestock production. By the end of the 1880s, there were over five million sheep and more than one million cattle in New Mexico, ranging freely over open ranges; numbers stayed high into the 1920s. (In contrast, today there are only 1.6 million cattle and sheep total in New Mexico.) This intense, landscape-wide grazing apparently

For example, some ponderosa pine stands now have well over 2,000 stems per acre, in contrast to 120 years ago when only about 50 stems per acre were present. Piñon-juniper woodlands are also characterized by higher tree densities today, contributing to losses in herbaceous vegetation cover and associated increases in soil erosion (note that recent U.S. Forest Service inventory data

Prescribed fire. (Photo courtesy of Don Usner.)

reduced the grassy fuels to the point that surface fires ceased to spread, inadvertently resulting in *de facto* fire suppression. Active fire suppression by the U.S. Forest Service became an emphasis after 1910, as woody fuels and forest densities began to build up. Today over a million dollars are spent in an average year to fight fires in the Jemez Mountains alone (the 1996 Dome Fire cost around $10 million), and the cost of fire suppression in the West is now averaging almost $1 billion a year!

Tree rings also record how local forests have changed over the past century since the widespread surface fires ceased. Age studies show increasing numbers of trees establishing during the 20th century in most forest types, ranging from ponderosa pine and mixed conifer forests down through piñon-juniper woodlands.

indicate the presence of about 1.4 billion piñon trees in New Mexico). These great increases in tree density in multiple vegetation types have caused declines in herbaceous under-stories, as the grasses are choked by the shade, needle mats, and competition from the dominant trees.

As a result of these changes in vegetation and fuels, fire suppression during this century has promoted conditions that today threaten New Mexico's forests with increasingly large, intense, and uncontrollable crown fires. The past 20 years have been unusually wet in our region, but true drought conditions (like the 1950s) will certainly recur unless global climate has indeed changed recently. The Dome and Hondo Fires that took place after the dry winter of 1996 are just a small foreshadowing of the potential for enormous and unnaturally intense wildfires to burn through our overcrowded forests and woodlands when multi-year drought returns. Such large crown fires will have many undesirable ecological and social effects, from degradation of habitats for endangered species to downstream flooding of human settlements.

## Summary

Most forests, woodlands, and grasslands in northern New Mexico evolved with frequent, low-intensity fires. The removal of the natural process of fire by human suppression has disrupted these ecosystems in many ways, including the loss of much grassy vegetation as woody plants have expanded in distribution and increased in density.

Many local forests, woodlands, and grasslands need to be restored to more open conditions to protect both ecological values and human communities, and research has been proceeding on environmentally sensitive ways to effectively implement restoration treatments. While site-specific conditions must always be carefully considered, general examples of ecologically appropriate restoration efforts include: cutting and burning trees out of invaded grasslands and meadows; thinning and prescribed burning of ponderosa pine forests to reduce the density of understory trees; and thinning younger piñon and juniper from thick woodlands, using the slash to mulch the eroding interspaces between remnant trees.

One outcome of such restoration efforts would be a shift in ecological dominance back toward the natural pattern of more abundant herbaceous vegetation in most local ecosystems. While not the primary motivation for most ecosystem restoration efforts, it is possible that the widespread restoration of enhanced grassy vegetation could help resolve persistent range management conflicts on public lands by providing additional grazing capacity on upland settings, away from the environmental conflicts associated with grazing in riparian zones.

Piñon-juniper encroachment at Sid Goodloe's Carrizo Valley Ranch. (Photo courtesy of Sid Goodloe.)

*The views expressed here are those of the author and do not represent*

# Forging a West that Works:

*an official position of the USGS.*

Where Have All the Grasslands Gone?

# Wet Meadows: Like Money in the Bank

*by Bill Zeedyk*

**B**ill Zeedyk owns and operates a small consulting business specializing in the restoration of wetland and riparian habitats using "low tech," hands-on methods and native materials. Bill holds a B.S. degree in Forestry (Wildlife Management) from the University of New Hampshire. Bill retired from the U.S. Forest Service in 1990 after 34 years. His career included assignments as research forester, assistant district ranger, forest wildlife biologist, staff officer for wildlife and watershed management, endangered species biologist, and finally staff director for wildlife and wisheries management, Southwestern Region, Albuquerque, where he served for 14 years. Following retirement, Bill soon realized that a life of leisure was not for him. As he puts it, "I couldn't be happy doing nothing." So gradually, he began to develop a second career focusing on simple techniques for stabilizing and restoring incised stream channels and gullied wetlands on public and private lands in the Southwest and Mexico. Successful projects include Rio Galisteo, Largo Creek, and Dry Cimarron Creek in New Mexico, the Rio Laja in Guanajato, Mexico and Nutrioso Creek, Pueblo Colorado Wash, and Tsailee Creek in Arizona, as well as wetlands in the Zuni Mountains, the Valle Vidal, Buell Park, and Cebolla Canyon. Bill likes to share what he knows with others and has conducted numerous hands-on training workshops featuring his own low-tech measures utilizing readily available native materials. His workshops have been sponsored by various state, federal, and tribal agencies as well as non-profit organizations such as The Quivira Coalition, New Mexico Riparian Council, National Audubon Society, The Nature Conservancy, Edgewood Soil and Conservation District, University of Missouri, and others. In support of the workshops Bill has prepared several field manuals including *Managing Roads for Wet Meadow Ecosystem Recovery*, a publication for which he received a national award in wetlands conservation from Ducks Unlimited and the Forest Service. Bill is a life-long member of the Wildlife Society and is a Certified Wildlife Biologist. He is a member of the Society of Wetland Scientists, past president of New Mexico Riparian Council, vice president of Albuquerque Wildlife Federation, and vice president of Intermountain Conservation Trust.

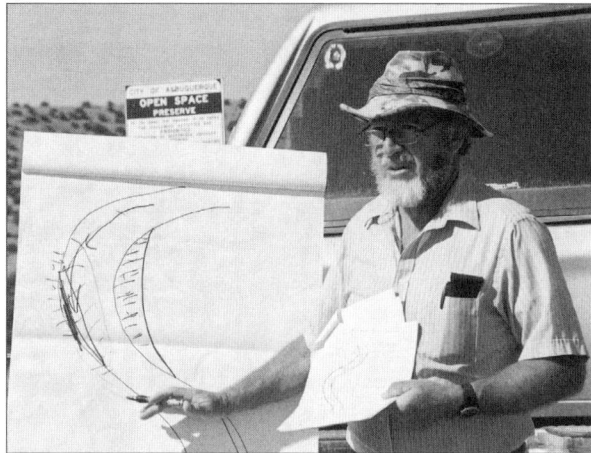

Wet meadows are like money in the bank, a nest egg tucked away for a rainy day or a drought year.

Wet meadows produce higher forage yields than adjacent upland pastures, up to 25 times as much, if well stocked with deep-rooted native wet soil species such as sedges,

Bill's "one-rock" dams are used for water harvesting. (All photos courtesy of Courtney White, unless otherwise indicated.)

rushes, and wet soil grasses. Wet meadows with wet soil plants can yield up to five times the forage of sites stocked with shallow-rooted Kentucky bluegrass.

Cattle are naturally attracted to the palatable, nutritious, and succulent greenery found in wet areas. High in protein and vitamins, this early forage is also highly attractive to wildlife, especially deer, elk, and wild geese.

## Values

Wet meadows provide many values to society and the natural world. As a subset of riparian habitats, wet meadows are key habitats for many different species of plants and wildlife. Their beauty and tranquility offer attractive and restful settings for camping, hiking, and picnicking. Wet meadows are ideal outdoor classrooms for nature study, bird watching, botanizing, and wildlife photography.

Gentle slopes, deep soils, and dense vegetation are factors that make wet meadows valuable in providing natural flood control. Most wet meadows are located in flatter portions of valleys where some natural structure has caused sediments to collect over time. When flood flows streaming off steeper slopes reach these more level areas, they spread out, lose speed and energy, and percolate into the soil to recharge the shallow alluvial water table. Not only are flood crests lowered and delayed, the stored ground water maintains stream base flows through the dry season. In the process, sediments, toxic substances, and nutrients are removed from the water column and stored in the vegetation or soil.

One natural value of wet meadows that everyone appreciates is wildlife habitat. Because they stay moist and are rich in nutrients, wet meadows are key habitat for both riparian dependent and upland species of wildlife. Brewers blackbirds nest along their margins. Wild turkey hens bring their broods of young poults to the edges to feed on grass seeds and grasshoppers which are a rich source of calcium and protein vitally needed to support the growth of bones, muscle, and feathers. Violet-green swallows sweep back and forth patrolling for midges, moths, and other insects that they carry back to their young hidden in nesting cavities in nearby pine snags.

## Savings for Drought

Wet meadows are a reliable source of nutritious forage for cattle and wild-life, even during drought years like 1990, 1996, or 2000. Sometimes the only available forage during drought years is that occurring on wetland sites, wet meadows, playas, cienegas, and riparian areas. Fly over New Mexico's parched forests and rangelands in a drought year, and you will see the wet soil areas sparkling like emeralds against the dry, brown landscape.

But a wet meadow, like a savings account in the bank, is not much use in the hard times if it has been drawn down during the good times.

Some impacts that draw down the productivity of wet mead-ows are back-to-back growing season use, season-long grazing, short residual stubble heights at the end of grazing, soil compaction, livestock trailing, improperly drained roads and travel ways, expanding erosion fans, and invading exotic or upland vegetation.

What is puzzling to me is why some ranchers struggle to restore degraded upland pastures capable of producing only 200 to 400 pounds of forage per acre while continuing to ignore the declining condition of wetland sites capable of producing

Bill [left] conducting a workshop on riparian restoration techniques.

4,000 to 5,000 pounds of forage per acre, especially when the wetter sites are easier to restore.

## Some Key Concepts

1. Moist soil vegetation requires more water than falls directly on site as precipitation. The extra water must get there from some-where else. It arrives as overland flow from adjacent uplands, as overbank flow spilling from stream channels during storm events or spring snow-melt, as subsurface flow moving through the shallow, alluvial water table, or as deep groundwater welling from springs and seeps. There are no other natural sources. Any land disturbance which blocks or dimin-

Bill and Van Clothier using a model creek to demonstrate the principle of "induced meandering." (Photo courtesy of Tamara Sherburn.)

aerated soil conditions; high or low soil pH; high salinity or other factors. What is more, many wetland grasses and grass-like species possess long, fibrous, or rhizomatous root systems that tunnel through the soil and open up passageways for overflowing surface water to infiltrate and percolate through the soil quickly. Wetland species usually propagate themselves both by seed and vegetatively (rhizome, corms, bulbs, and stem parts). Flood waters tend to spread such propagules widely across wetland sites assuring rapid colonization of such areas when favorable conditions exist.

3. Moist soil areas wetted by periodic runoff from adjacent hill slopes tend to exhibit patterns of shallow, low-velocity sheeting that spread evenly across the wet meadow. Maintaining a fairly dense, vigorous stand of sedges and wetland grasses aids in this process. Each and every grass stem, whether dead or alive, erect or prostrate, acts like a tiny dam that impedes, slows, spreads, and disperses the flow across the land. This assures that every part of the land is wetted each time significant runoff occurs.

If a meadow has been grazed too closely and left without sufficient residual stubble, the sheeting flow effect is reduced and surface runoff is quickly lost downslope. Likewise, any unnatural disturbances to the smooth plane of the wet meadow surface, such as wheel ruts, cattle trails, ditches, berms, or gullies, tend to concentrate and accelerate surface

ishes the volume of surface or subsurface flow reaching a wet soil area will diminish the productivity of wetland areas whether wet meadow, cienega, playa, or riparian area.

2. Moist soil areas naturally support a variety of specially adapted wet soil plants whose adaptations suit them to the unique environmental conditions common to the local area of concern. These adaptations include: length of the flooding period during which soils remain saturated; the ability to grow, propagate, and survive during alternate periods of well aerated and poorly

runoff rather than slow and disperse it. As a result, increasingly larger areas dry out and convert to upland species.

4. Stream channels lose water to adjacent wetlands both as overbank flow and as subsurface flow oozing through the stream-side soil. Gravity pulls the overbank flow down into the fine-grained surface soil, but capillary action pulls it both upward from the shallow groundwater and laterally from the streambank.

Capillary action in fine-grained silty or loamy soil can lift water as high as 40 inches above the alluvial water table but, if the soil profile is made up of coarse-grained particles (gravel, pebbles, or sand), capillary water will rise only a few inches. A lens of coarse-grained material sandwiched in the soil strata will interrupt the flow of capillary water just as surely as a light switch breaks the flow of electricity. Therefore, it is critical that subsurface flows can reach up to the capillary zone to maintain meadow productivity. That is why maintaining a healthy, meandering stream channel which has not become too deeply entrenched is critical to maintaining a healthy wet meadow grassland.

An indication that a former wetland site no longer receives sufficient surface or subsurface moisture is apparent in the replace-

ment of wetland plants by invading rubber rabbitbrush, shrubby cinquefoil, ring pussy toe, grama grass, pines, or junipers. These species

Wet meadow areas on a restored section of Largo Creek.

cannot survive in periodically saturated soil.

## Strategies for Keeping Wet Meadows Healthy

There are several strategies which a concerned rancher might use to build up the ready reserve in his or her wet meadow account.

1. Reduce the use of wetland and riparian areas during normal or wet years, so that wet soil plants can move into and fully occupy potentially suitable soil types and build healthy root systems to sustain themselves through dry cycles.

2. If an intensive grazing system is not in effect which places special emphasis on the productivity of wet soil areas, fence wetland and riparian areas into a separate pasture or pastures, for more intensive

Volunteers constructing "baffles" and "riffles" on Largo Creek during a Riparian Restoration Workshop.

management. Closely limit stocking and the duration of the grazing period, so that the pasture receives uniform grazing pressure and that a residual stubble height of eight inches remains when livestock are removed. This will ensure an adequate thatch to slow and disperse surface runoff, especially snowmelt.

3. A third strategy is to inspect the land for apparent irregularities in the drainage pattern and correct any fixable problems. Surface features which may result in a loss of wet soil productivity include entrenched roads and travel ways that capture and direct water out of or away from the meadow surface. Roadside ditches or berms, poorly placed culvert locations on stream crossings or culverts installed too deeply, livestock trailing, old or abandoned ditch systems, terraces or berms, livestock tanks, and pit tanks that funnel water out of the wet soil area may also result in a loss of wet soil productivity.

4. A final strategy is to install stream channel improvements that raise the streambed elevation or increase the sinuosity of meandering stream channels and lower stream channel gradient so that storm runoff does not run off so quickly.

This doesn't mean damming up or diverting the river! Modifying stream/road crossing culverts is one way of returning an eroded stream channel or gully to its proper elevation relative to the meadow surface. Removing the culvert and installing a porous road-fill embankment is another. A more radical method is to completely replace an eroded stream channel with a redesigned and reconstructed channel. Obviously, such endeavors require skilled professionals and appropriate permitting from regulatory agencies, but they can have big payoffs in terms of restored productivity of wetland and riparian pastures.

To sum up, wet meadows are highly productive. If healthy, they have a good deal of resilience to withstand occasional heavy grazing pressure in drought years if allowed to recover during more normal conditions. They are like money in the bank. Are you doing everything you can to keep your account growing so it will be there when you need it?

# The Urbanization of Ranching

*by Nathan F. Sayre*

Nathan Sayre is a college assistant professor at New Mexico State University and the Jornada Experimental Range. He holds a Ph.D. in Anthropology from the University of Chicago. He is the author of *The New Ranch Handbook: A Guide to Restoring Western Rangelands* (The Quivira Coalition, 2001) and *Ranching, Endangered Species, and Urbanization in the Southwest: Species of Capital* (University of Arizona Press, 2002). Nathan has worked with The Quivira Coalition, the Altar Valley Conservation Alliance, the Sonoran Desert Conservation Plan's Ranch Conservation Technical Advisory Team, and the Malpai Borderlands Group.

The phrase "cows vs. condos" is frequently used to summarize the debate over ranching and environmentalism in the West today. It suggests a simple opposition: either a piece of land will be a ranch, or it will be developed as residential real estate. Each new subdivision lends support to this view. But the dynamics of land use change are more complex than this simple phrase suggests, particularly as regards environmental issues. The "urbanization of ranching" is less rhetorically elegant, perhaps, but it better captures the processes by which ranch lands, previously valued according to their capacity to produce cattle, have come to be valued according to their potential as residential real estate. This shift in valuation has environ-

mental consequences even before a ranch is subdivided. It has occurred at different times in different places; I focus here on southern Arizona, where the urbanization of ranching can be dated to about 1970.

## Background: The Cattle Boom

It is important to review historical events which established the economic and ecological framework for modern ranching. Between 1873 and 1893, the cattle boom spread rapidly across the western United States. In Arizona, cattle numbers exploded from about 40,000 in 1870 to 1.5 million in 1891. An extended drought from 1891 to 1893 resulted in massive die-offs and irreparable damage to rangelands. In the aftermath of the boom, government studies emphasized the role of the open range system in creating the conditions for overgrazing. The public domain was exploited by everyone, because no one could effectively regulate its use; "free grass" inevitably created a tragedy of the commons.

Grazing leases were instituted to remedy this situation. Culminating in the Taylor Grazing Act of 1934, lease systems recognized in law what John Wesley Powell had argued in his 1878 *Report on the Lands of the Arid Region of the United States*: the Western range was too arid for farming and should therefore be managed for livestock grazing. Two

## "The disparity between grazing and suburban land values creates a strong incentive to convert ranches into suburbia wherever possible."

premises informed this position: first, that most of the range would never find a higher economic use than grazing; second, that secure, individual tenure was necessary to give ranchers incentive to conserve range resources.

The cattle boom had capitalized on natural bounty for short-term economic gain, resulting in long-term ecological damage. Repairing that damage would require a long-term commitment to range improvement. Ranchers could only

be expected to make such an investment if they could be confident of long-term returns in the form of improved forage conditions.

### Highest But Unprofitable Use

Grazing leases stabilized the livestock industry by institutionalizing a compromise between the arid ecosystem and capitalist economics. Throughout the frontier period, prominent Americans such as Teddy Roosevelt had assumed that ranching would be superceded by agriculture and then industry in a sort of evolutionary sequence. Leases conceded that this was mistaken, that grazing was the only way to make money on millions of acres of lands ecologically unsuited for tillage agriculture.

Viewed from the vantage of the rest of the economy, however, grazing represented a comparatively unprofitable land use. In 1930, for example, the taxable per-acre value of grazing lands in Pima County was $2.57, while the value of suburban and irrigated lands was $57.38 and $52.24, respectively.[1] This disparity persists today, officially recognized in property tax schedules, state trust land lease rates, and appraisal methods. The two land uses participate in entirely different markets. For grazing, the value of a piece of land is a function of its carrying capacity and the price of beef on national and international markets. Viewed as residential real estate, land value is determined by the supply and demand for housing, influenced by local, regional, and national factors.

The disparity between grazing and suburban land values creates a strong incentive to convert ranches into suburbia wherever possible.

## Improving Livestock Production

Prior to about 1970, the assumption that grazing was the highest economic use of southern Arizona rangelands held true. Based on this assumption, ranchers, range scientists, and government agencies focused attention on improving conditions for livestock production. Improved breeding increased the quality and value of beef, enabling smaller herds to yield equivalent money returns. Fences were necessary for controlled breeding, and gave ranchers greater control over their herds. Wells and stocktanks distributed water over the range so that grasses could be more evenly utilized. Beginning in the 1910s and accelerating after the Depression, erosion control measures were instituted: spreader dams, contour embankments, canyon reservoirs, and reseeding projects aimed to retain water and topsoil. The spread of mesquite and consequent crowding out of grasses prompted chaining, chemical defoliation, and reseeding programs, especially after 1955. All of these programs represented capital investments, which (with the exception of

breeding) endured in the land. They were expensive and made economic sense only over the long term. A variety of state and federal tax incentives and cost-sharing programs were implemented to encourage ranchers to undertake range improvements which otherwise appeared too long-term or too uncertain to justify the costs.

Quemado, New Mexico. (Photo courtesy of Courtney White.)

## Ecological Condition Improved, Somewhat

Twentieth century investments have improved the ecological condition of the range relative to conditions in the 1890s, but they have not succeeded in restoring pre-cattle boom health or productivity. Early researchers reported that as little as three years of complete rest would be sufficient to restore desert grasslands to their pre-boom carrying capacity.[2] Unfortunately, this proved overly optimistic.

Certain ecological changes, most notably arroyo formation and downcutting, cannot be reversed and may have far-reaching effects on vegetation. Others, such as mesquite invasion, have largely eluded remediation efforts. Relative to "original" conditions, southern

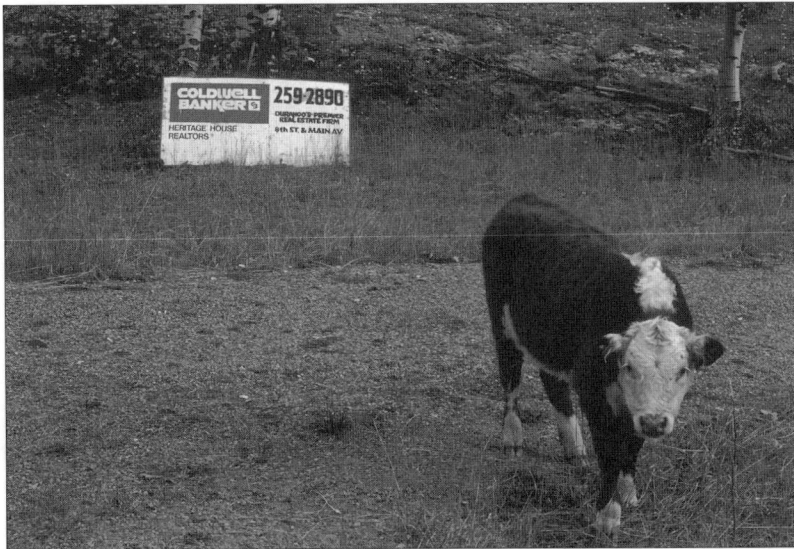

(Photo courtesy of Courtney White.)

Arizona ranges are today shrub-dominated, whether due to grazing pressure, fire exclusion, or other causes such as climate change.

Even shrubs and mesquite are preferable to bare ground, however, and bare ground is what can be seen in photographs from the 1890s and early 1900s. The Bureau of Land Management's 1990 observation that rangelands are in better condition now than at any time this century—much decried by environmentalists—is accurate, albeit carefully worded.[3] Perhaps more significantly, some ranges in southern Arizona have improved markedly while others appear nearly unchanged from a

century ago, suggesting that investments in range restoration have had significant effects on ecosystem health. The Buenos Aires Ranch, for example, was so dramatically altered by range improvement measures in the 1970s that the U.S. Fish and Wildlife Service deemed it worthy of acquisition as a National Wildlife Refuge.

Wholesale revegetation of desert grasslands for grazing purposes came to an end in the 1970s, for a variety of reasons. Rising oil prices made chaining more expensive. Chemical defoliation of mesquite proved less successful than initially hoped. Environmental regulations on herbicides and endangered species created bureaucratic obstacles. Overall, ranchers and rangeland specialists came to the conclusion that revegetation was uneconomical: the costs could not be justified in view of the fact that "revegetation success is largely determined by the pattern of summer precipitation in a given year."[4]

### 1970s: Urbanization Supplants Cattle

This judgment cannot be understood apart from the larger economics of land use in the region, however. What is economical, after all, depends on opportunity costs, and the opportunity costs of ranching were changing rapidly.

In the past 30 years, urbanization has supplanted cattle as the standard of value for ranches in southern Arizona. Around 1958, southern Arizona entered a period of appreciating real estate values, which has continued almost uninterrupted to the present day. Cold War defense spending, post-World War II prosperity, and the widespread availability of air conditioning and automobiles attracted people to Arizona in huge numbers. State population increased 74% during the 1950s, and another 36% in the 1960s; from 1970 to 1997 it increased another 250%.

While population growth has concentrated on the fringes of Phoenix and Tucson, its effects on rural land values have been much more widespread. Well ahead of actual construction, speculators ventured into rural areas, bidding up the price of land and making plans for subdivision. In the 1960s, Arizona became notorious for the fraudulent practices of speculative real estate developers. In 1966 alone, 302 subdivisions were recorded with a total of 32,000 individual lots (*Arizona Daily Star*, 17 March 1966). By 1972, University of Arizona professor of urban planning Robert Carpenter could report:

"Proposed or in various stages of construction are 55 large-scale land-conversion projects, many of them labeled new communities, of a thousand acres and over. The total area involved is in excess of 643,000 acres. . . .The vast majority of the projects are programmed for lot sales in a speculative land market that is nationwide." (*Arizona Daily Star*, 11 October 1972)

Speculation issued directly from the gap between land values for cattle production and those for residential homes. In the case of the 55,000-acre Rio Rico development, for example:

"General Acceptance Corp.'s predecessor, Gulf American Corp., bought the Baca Float ranch for a reported $3.5 million, or about $64 an acre. GAC is now selling an acre for an average of $3,000. Like the Baca Float ranch, most Arizona developments are on what was once considered prime grazing land." (*Arizona Daily Star*, 26 December 1971)

Tax policies crafted to encourage ranchers to invest in range improvements provided further incentive to speculation. Under the federal income tax code, improvements could be amortized as capital investments, usually on a seven-year schedule. According to people involved at the time, improvements sometimes approached the full market value of the ranch, meaning that almost all of one's investment was sheltered. Moreover, until the 1980s, one could use losses in ranching to write off income in other pursuits. Additionally, state property tax laws assess ranch lands at a fraction of the rate for commercial and residential lands. Wealthy individuals and corporations flocked to invest assets from other enterprises in ranches, where the initial face value could be amortized, even as the market value of the land was appreci-

ating at well above the rate of infla-
tion.

## Urbanization Accelerates as Ranching Ecnomics Decline

Throughout the '70s and

Colorado. (Photo courtesy of Dan Dagget.)

'80s, urbanization accelerated in lockstep with the deterioration of economic conditions for cattle ranching. In 1980, the *Daily Star* reported:

"The price of land for residential use in Tucson increased by as much as 150 percent in the past 18 months, a local real-estate specialist said yesterday." (1 February)

Early in 1981, the *Tucson Citizen* ran a story on the purchase of a ranch in the Avra Valley, northwest of Tucson, which illustrates well the practices of land conversion:

"Ronald D. Cohn, . . .recently took control of about 15,000 acres of ranch land in the valley,

14,000 of which is grazing land owned by the government and leased . . . . 'I think the land has a lot of great potential,' [Cohn] said. . . .Cohn said the land, most of which made up Robles' Agua Blanca Ranch, attracted him not only as a speculative investment but also because of tax advantages and what he called a 'lifelong dream' of owning a working cattle ranch. 'It has 130 head of cattle on it right now and I want to keep it a working ranch for the time being,' he said. 'But there's no question in my mind that the Avra Valley will fill up with people. I'd like to put together a decent residential project, ranchettes maybe. . . .It will be a nice setting for people who value a rural lifestyle, and it's only a 30-minute drive from the corner of Ina and Oracle roads,' he said." (21 March)

While outsiders' capital propped up ranch values, this was a mixed blessing to "established ranchers [who] are caught in somewhat of a financial squeeze. While costs of farm supplies have doubled or tripled in the last decade, prices of farm commodities have remained virtually the same." (*Arizona Daily Star*, 7 January 1983) Agricultural economics undermined profitability at the same time that rising land values increased initial investment costs and assessed valuations. A 1983 study found that an average 300-cow ranch in Arizona was worth at least $500,000, while income was $5,485, or 1% on investment (*Arizona Daily Star*, 20 November 1983). Today, according to experienced cattlemen, a good ranch can pay off a mortgage of about $50 per acre, but even remote properties in southern Arizona are valued at $200 per acre and up.[5] Not surprisingly, banks have shown an increasingly strong preference for residential over ranch mortgages. Not only are returns per acre much higher, but suburbanites' ability to pay off their mortgages is independent of the fickle climate.

### Economic and Ecological Dilemma

Urbanization confronts ranchers with a dilemma at once economic and ecological. Economically, they must decide if and when to sell out. "Land rich and cash poor," as they sometimes describe themselves, they do not face outright bankruptcy (like midwestern farmers). If money were their only concern, they might consider themselves lucky. But for most, putting a price on their livelihood is a moral predicament, especially if they come from longstanding ranching families. Ecologically, urbanization undermines the original premise of stewardship—namely, that rangelands will remain in grazing indefinitely.

The prospect that one's ranch will sooner or later become a subdivision, and that for such a purpose the health of the range is irrelevant,

> "Ecologically, urbanization undermines the original premise of stewardship—namely, that rangelands will remain in grazing indefinitely. The prospect that one's ranch will sooner or later become a subdivision, and that for such a purpose the health of the range is irrelevant, makes it rational to abandon long-term stewardship in favor of shorter-term profits."

makes it rational to abandon long-term stewardship in favor of shorter-term profits. Thus the economic pressures of urbanization have environmental consequences for ranching even before ranches are subdivided.

### Cultural Dimension

The urbanization of ranching is not only an economic and ecological phenomenon; the cultural dimension is perhaps the most conspicuous and puzzling. Many subdivisions are called "ranches," sometimes retaining the names of the cattle operations they displace. Moreover, the putative values of the "ranching lifestyle"— wide open spaces, starry skies, the deer and the antelope, etc. etc.—are prominent features in the promotion of large subdivisions. The following newspaper advertisement is representative:

"Escalante is the newest offering of the incomparable Dragoon Mountain Ranch—a low density gated community of approximately 400 ranchsites set amid a sprawling 18,000 acre reserve. The ranchland . . .is diverse and alluring; lush foothills vegetation, gently terracing hills, rich meadows. . . ,

"Politically, the real estate boom, like the cattle boom a century ago, demonstrates that the most lucrative lines of economic activity typically elude effective government regulation until the natural bounty that they exploit has been exhausted."

rich soils, abundant pure water and equestrian trails. . . . The view . . .is spectacular; wilderness mountain ranges surround the Ranch, with the spectacular 52,000 acre Coronado National Forest hugging the Ranch. Wildlife is abundant and exotic. The nearby San Pedro River attracts over 300 species of birds to the area. Deer, fox, coatimundi, blue heron and others are frequent visitors. Build your dream-vacation-retirement-retreat at Escalante where your lifestyle is protected for now and for

the future. . . ."

Many environmentalists portray Arizona rangelands as permanently and drastically degraded by cattle grazing. If this is the case, it is odd that Dragoon Mountain Ranch, carved from lands grazed continuously for more than a century, can be promoted as "diverse," "lush," and teeming with "abundant and exotic" wildlife. It need hardly be pointed out that subdividing the "ranch" into 400-odd homesites will likely have a negative impact on the very wildlife being invoked to promote it.

The urbanization of ranching recapitulates the 19th century cattle boom in key respects. Economically, it capitalizes on a "free" feature of the environment, namely the mild climate and romanticized "nature" so attractive to retirees, tourists, and so-called New Westerners. Ecologically, it carves up open spaces and poses a threat that is at once less visible and more profound than grasses and vegetation: water supplies for a population far larger than the area has ever sustained. The depth to reach water in wells in the Tucson basin has increased steadily since the 1930s, and groundwater pumping today is approximately nine times what it was then.[6] The Central Arizona Project only postpones the problem—it does not resolve it.

Politically, the real estate boom, like the cattle boom a century ago, demonstrates that the most lucrative lines of economic activity typically elude effective government regulation until the natural bounty that they exploit has been exhausted.

Recognizing that some environmentalists are attempting to confront urban sprawl, it is nevertheless worth posing the question: given that the worst damage of grazing is now 100 years old, is it mere coincidence that the environmentalist critique of ranching emerged at the same time that ranchlands became valuable for urbanization?

**Notes:**

1. C.B. Brown and C.J. McCash, "Program for Conservation of Runoff Water and Water Investigations." In the *Annual Report of the Pima County Agricultural Extension Service for the period 12/1/30-12/1/31,* located in the Arizona Historical Society files, Tucson, Arizona.

2. David Griffiths, "A Protected Stock Range in Arizona." *U.S.D.A Bureau of Plant Industry Bulletin no. 177,* April 19, 1910.

3. U.S. Department of the Interior, Bureau of Land Management, "State of the Public Rangelands: 1990." See also U.S. General Accounting Office, "Public Rangelands: Some Riparian Areas Restored but Widespread Improvement Will Be Slow" *(GAO/RCED 88-105),* which observes that "[s]ince this period of rapid deterioration [1880-1900], the overall condition of western rangeland has stabilized and, in places, improved." (p.8)

4. Bruce A. Roundy and Sharon H. Biedenbender, "Revegetation in the Desert Grassland," in Mitchel P. McClaran and Thomas R. Van Devender, eds., *The Desert Grassland* (Tucson: University of Arizona Press, 1995), p.294.

5. The ratio of deeded to leased acres is of course critical in determining the pressures of urbanization for any particular ranch. A great deal depends on appraisers and lenders, who gauge the market and judge whether to value a ranch for its cattle production or its residential potential.

6. Barbara Tellman et al., *Arizona's Changing Rivers: How People Have Affected the Rivers* (Tucson: Water Resources Research Center, College of Agriculture, University of Arizona, March 1997), pp.21-22.

# Pursuing the Trickster: Monitoring as a Paradigm for Change in the West

*by Will Barnes*

Will Barnes is a "recovering lawyer" who went back to school and recently earned a M.S. in Biology from the University of New Mexico. Today he runs his own consulting firm, called Grasswork, Inc., which provides ecological monitoring services. Clients include The Conservation Fund's Valle Grande Grass Bank, located on Rowe Mesa near Santa Fe, and the Valles Caldera National Preseve, near Los Alamos, New Mexico.

Last week I found myself setting out on foot across the Valle Grande, the largest caldera in the new Valles Caldera National Preserve. Located in the Jemez Mountains of northern New Mexico, the Valle Grande is an open, bowl-shaped mountain grassland, some 12 miles in circumference. As I stood on the road above the valley floor, looking out toward the area I had already designated as a potential monitoring site, I saw in the distance a pair of coyotes zig-zagging through the grass—now stopping, now in a trot, sometimes near to each other, sometimes moving apart, seemingly hunting—and I thought to myself, OK, they have it right, that is just where I need to be. So I followed the coyotes into the valley, until I came to what I hope will be the perfect location, representing just the right eco-variation in the landscape. This will be one of approximately 35 permanent rangeland monitoring sites across the Valles Caldera. As I finished confirming the soil type and mapping the site on my GPS unit, something made me look up—there I was sitting shoulder-deep in Arizona fescue, mountain muhly, and the yellowing, inscrutable sedges, alone, in the middle of this wide valley, the road barely visible—my coyotes had gone and the sky was enormous. I lay back in the grass and laughed, how in the world did I get here?

---

### Circuitous Route

Perhaps I have been following coyotes far longer than I have realized—the route has been circuitous,

Monitoring training at a Quivira workshop. (Photo courtesy of Courtney White.)

to say the least, and it's a story about monitoring, though it starts in a law office. In the spring of 1989, fresh out of law school, I had just begun my practice as an attorney. Thinking that water law meant walking ditches, and that environmental law meant that I could be out on the ground learning about erosion and wild animals and open spaces, I set up shop in Santa Fe, intending to advocate for the environment. One of the first calls to my new office was from my uncle who had recently bought a ranch in Arizona. As it happened, the property was about an hour's drive north of Wickenberg—70,000 acres of mixed State/BLM land along the Santa Maria—pristine, desert river country. In addition, half the BLM portion of the allotment was in a Wilderness Study

Area. The grazing preference was for 240 CYLs (Cows Year-Long).

As soon as the transfer to my uncle went through, it was appealed by the Environmental Law Clinic at Arizona State University. The challenge was based on the argument that 240 CYLs would have a significant impact on the environment and that, under NEPA, an environmental impact statement was required prior to authorization of the grazing rights. This was not exactly what I had in mind when I had decided to practice environmental law, but my uncle was desperate, and it was my first real case.

So I made my way to Phoenix to meet with the BLM and to see the ranch. When I sat down with the supervisor, my first question was, "What evidence do you have? How do you know what the impact of 240 CYLs will be?" Immediately, though I did not know it at the time, we were talking about monitoring.

### Little Hard Data

What I found was that, overall, they had very little hard data to support their decision. On the BLM land, there was a series of less than ten photo points which had not been re-taken for at least ten years. There was rumor of a Parker Three-Step monitoring site, but no one was quite sure where it was, or when it had last been collected. The State lands had a series of species richness quadrats, but they also had not been collected in recent years. Finally, they had utilization analyses, but these had not been collected for three years, as the ranch had not been grazed during the sale period.

The monitoring in place on the Santa Maria ranch was not comprehensive in any way—either in terms of landscape coverage, or in terms of the kinds of data collected. In addition, the data they did have was mostly qualitative rather than quantitative; it was based on informal rancher and range-con assessment, knowledge of historic practices, and agency experience with other similarly situated ranches.

Nor was monitoring coordinated between state and federal lands, or with ranching activities, or with any of the various environmental groups. There was no overarching monitoring policy. There was no coordinated design for the monitoring program. There were no goals. There was no one person who was in charge of monitoring. As a result, monitoring was not on anyone's schedule—ten years might pass without anyone noticing that no monitoring had been completed.

## War of Conjecture

At first, as a good young attorney, I was thrilled. There were two reasons: One, there was no negative evidence against us—no proof from this particular piece of ground that grazing was harmful. And two, all the evidence they had was utterly assailable. We could challenge anything. It was subjective and there was hardly any of it. What this meant was that we could go out and find our own experts to prove whatever it was we wanted to prove. And we did that. For example, we were able to find a desert tortoise expert who was able to say that, in his years of experience and research, in fact, grazing was the best thing since toast for desert tortoise habitat.

What we learned quickly was that the lack of evidence cuts both ways. Of course, our worthy adversaries found their own desert tortoise expert, who said just the opposite—that, in fact, cattle grazing is really quite harmful to the desert tortoise. We were in a war of conjecture: We were making up what we thought must be happening on the ground to support what we hoped to achieve—that is, a viable cattle ranch. Yet, we had no idea what was actually happening in this particular place. As a result, we found all the evidence we could about ranches that were similar to our ranch that said, "Grazing is great. Grazing works, it improves the habitat, it's good for this piece of ground." Our opponents did just the opposite. They went out and found all the ranches they could, all the research they could find, that said, "Grazing is the worst thing that you could possibly do here." So they stacked up their papers. We stacked up our papers, and we hoped that, in the end, our stack would be bigger

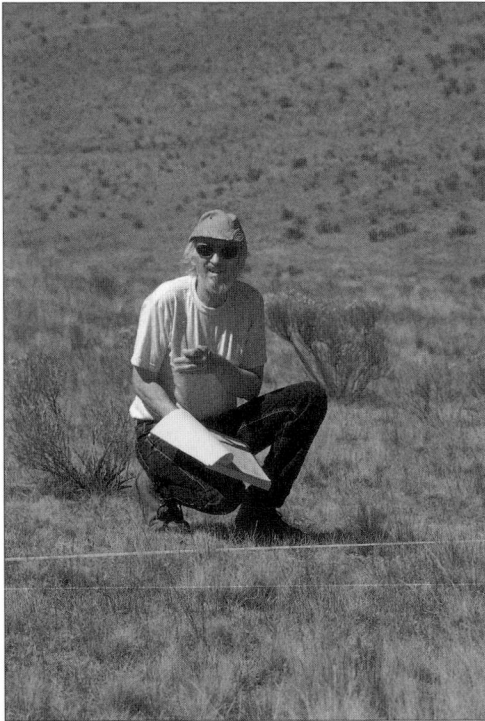

Quivira volunteer Mike Boring reading a monitoring transect at Vidal Creek in northern New Mexico. (Photo courtesy of Kirk Gadzia.)

than theirs. Realizing that it was going to take a long time for the BLM to sort this out, we thought in the interim that we should try to negotiate a solution. We had one of the most creative, energetic ranchers around. He was willing to try anything: herding, rotational grazing, riparian fencing. He just wanted to get out on the ground and start working. Unfortunately, however, the Environmental Law Clinic would not even come to the table so long as grazing was part of the equation. While we believed that good management could both mitigate and perhaps even eliminate environmental damage, they believed that cattle grazing, *per se*, was environmentally unsound. Our differences as to the root of the problem were so fundamental that we couldn't even begin to discuss solutions.

## Polarized

In the end, the whole process strongly polarized both sides. The briefs became more and more acrimonious. The parties refused to meet with each other. After about a

year, the BLM split the baby, authorizing 120 CYLs. All of us were angry, the environmentalists because they believed grazing in any form would be harmful to the fragile ecosystem, and my uncle because 120 CYLs was not financially feasible. Everyone appealed. After another year, we transferred the case to local Arizona counsel, and my uncle got a stay so that he could ranch pending the final outcome. The case is still in litigation—11 years later.

So what does this have to do with monitoring? For me at least, my uncle's ranch was another coyote. I followed for a while then found myself in a strange new country, my coyote having dissolved over some far ridge. Eventually, I ended up with a degree in biology and a job monitoring grasslands for the Conservation Fund, and now for the Valles Caldera National Preserve. What I keep thinking is that, if we had had the kind of quantified data that I'm collecting now, in my new career, the dialogue between my uncle, the Environmental Law Clinic, and the BLM would have been completely different. We would have circumvented the conjecture and blame game. Right from the start we would have had real data to talk about. We would have been able to say, "OK, look, in this riparian area we know we're going to lose willow and cottonwood and we're going to have more erosion. It's not going to work. You can't graze here." Or we might have been able to say, "If you look at these uplands, you can see that when we graze we get better grass, actually, and there's more diversity."

## Shared Language

Monitoring data would have given us a language, a shared, concrete set of findings to come together around and from which to begin a discussion. Rather than basing our conclusions on some guessed-at reality, our interpretations would have been based on actual measurements taken from that particular piece of ground. We would have been one whole step farther down the road, arguing about interpretations of data, rather than whether or not data even exist.

This is not to say that monitoring is just about litigation avoidance—it is useful for that—but there's more to it. Monitoring is the only way to know whether or not management decisions and land treatments have actually worked. It also provides a mechanism for testing new ideas, and it provides protection against bad decisions. It allows a land manager to say, "We don't know exactly what's going to happen here. But we're confident in our monitoring system so we can try it. We're going to put cows out, and we're going to watch what happens. If we see that there's too much erosion going on, we can change our management." Monitoring gives the manager a way to see what's going on, a way to spot trends, often before changes can be detected through more casual observation. It's a

mechanism for making better informed decisions and for managing before the crisis.

So what exactly does it mean to "monitor" something? I think of it as a "systematized watching" of the landscape. The two key components of any monitoring system are that it needs to be regular, and it needs to be recorded: The same measures or observations, using the same protocols, are taken from the same locations at the same times of year, and

> "Monitoring is the only way to know whether or not management decisions and land treatments have actually worked. It also provides a mechanism for testing new ideas, and it provides protection against bad decisions."

those measurements or observations are written down so that they can be remembered and compared.

There are a wide variety of monitoring methods and techniques, ranging from the highly quantitative to the highly qualitative. In recent years, efforts to systematize monitoring have focused on developing better quantitative methods. Data that are reduced to a set of precise numerical values or measurements are much easier to repeat, and to compare over time and between sample sets. It is also, therefore, much easier to use to pin-point differences, trends, and changes. Qualitative data is generally less

Monitoring. (Photo courtesy of Kris Havstad.)

expensive and less elaborate, but also less predictive and more subject to claims of bias.

**Long-Term Commitment**

Monitoring takes a long-term commitment. It takes patience. Results do not happen overnight. It also requires a variety of skills, from botany to soil science to ornithology, or to whatever it is being monitored. It also requires data management skills. Where will the data go? How will it be analyzed? How will it be reported? To whom will it be reported? These are complicated issues that need to be addressed as part of the monitoring process—it is not just about collecting data.

Depending on the situation, monitoring can be quite time and labor intensive. The type of moni-

toring selected should be based on management and monitoring goals, as well as on desired statistical resolution, desired repeatability, and financial and time constraints. In the long run, however, monitoring should be considered as an investment in the landscape. The costs of monitoring should be compared directly with the costs of not monitoring. For example, if the money spent on 11 years of litigation by all the parties in my uncle's case had been funneled instead into a monitoring program, we would have had the most highly monitored ranch in all the West. We would have been able to say now a great deal about the true impacts of grazing in that country.

**Working Together**

There would have been another benefit as well. In the time actually spent making enemies, we would have been working together on the ground to set monitoring goals and to collect and to report on our data. We would have been building a new community around the health of the land.

Personally, I believe that monitoring is here to stay. In my opinion, it needs to be as much a part of land management as the treatments are. There should be a monitoring department in each forest and BLM district. Monitoring should be afforded the same status as burning, or grazing, or cutting timber. The fact is that we cannot assess the success or failure of the burning and grazing and timber cutting of the past, because we have not adequately monitored. Today, we throw good money after bad, repeating projects, repeating efforts to remove encroaching piñon-juniper stands, for instance, that were begun in the '30s and again in the '50s and again in the '70s and again today because we did not adequately monitor the projects. We don't know what happened. We don't know why those past projects failed. Monitoring has been treated as the ugly stepsister. It has not been funded or even put into the budget. We say, "Okay, we're going to do this great burning project. We've got all these people who are experienced and ready to go for it. But we haven't set aside any extra money to do the monitoring." That has got to change. Monitoring needs the same infrastructure as any other management project. There have to be people that know how to collect the data, people to manage the data, people to run the monitoring program, and people to be held accountable.

## Impact

One of the problems is that monitoring is not glamorous. It is not as exciting as burning down a forest. It is not as exciting as cutting down trees. It is a much more daily kind of work. But I think, for that

very reason, monitoring can have a much greater impact on the way we live here in the West, and on the way that we look at our future. There is this idea first espoused by Aldo Leopold called "an ethic of place." How do we, as Westerners, acknowledge where we live, change our communities and our economies so that we become self-sufficient and self-sustaining? How do we put back what we've taken out of the ground and rehabilitate these places that we

> "The fact is that we cannot assess the success or failure of the burning and grazing and timber cutting of the past, because we have not adequately monitored."

live in? Maybe part of the answer is bringing together—instead of polarizing—the people who love pristine wilderness, and the people who make a living off the ground, and the people who drink the water that comes from the ground, and the people who eat the meat that comes off the ground. Maybe we bring all these people together to watch in a systematic way, to monitor the effects of their living on that ground—so that they might make decisions as a community about how to live better and how to become self-sustaining.

Monitoring, for me, is this wonderful activity. I get paid to watch the landscape change. One of the things that I notice is that there is a relationship between the observer and the observed. I have spent months looking daily at a particular grass, uncertain as to its true identity, until one day I notice the hairs at the ligule curving just so, in a way I had never noticed before, and it is like a name-tag, repeating itself over and over, literally shouting out its name to me. It is a profoundly intimate experience. And I realize that monitoring is about relationships: my relationship with this particular place and with these particular inhabitants. And I realize further that I have begun to care deeply about each of the places in which I have begun to monitor.

## Leap of Faith

If we take a leap of faith, like trusting the coyote to lead where we need to go, we might build monitoring associations, something akin to acequia associations, in which all the people with a stake in a particular landscape, come out together once a year to man the transects, to watch the birds and count the grasses. And then all that information would be funneled back to that year's major-domo, the Majordomo of Monitoring who would be responsible for writing a report and calling a meeting and saying to the people, "This is what we've learned this year. What are we going to do about it?"

I see monitoring as a kind of keystone for creating a new egalitarian community in the West, a com-munity that is much more aware of its relationships in and of the landscape. It would be a community much more capable of regulating itself and its impacts, because it would know first-hand and it would know intimately just what those impacts might be.